Figure 13 (see pages 20-21).
HOUSE IN SEATTLE, WASHINGTON (1909 WITH RECENT ADDITIONS).

Along BUNGALOW Lines

Creating an Arts & Crafts Home

PAUL DUCHSCHERER
Photography by Linda Svendsen

Gibbs Smith, Publisher
Salt Lake City

This book is dedicated to all those who admire, respect and help preserve America's historic architectural treasures, and also to those who transform the integrity and inspiration of period originals into new homes that honor our past, and will brighten our future.

First Edition
10 09 08 07 06   5 4 3 2 1

Text © 2006 Paul Duchscherer
Photographs © 2006 Linda Svendsen

Published by
Gibbs Smith, Publisher
P.O. Box 667
Layton, Utah 84041

1.800.748.5439 orders
www.gibbs-smith.com

Designed by Dawn DeVries Sokol
Printed and bound in Hong Kong

Library of Congress Cataloging-in-Publication Data

Duchscherer, Paul.
  Along bungalow lines : creating an arts & crafts style home / Paul
Duchscherer & Linda Svendsen.—1st ed.
     p. cm.
  Includes bibliographical references.
  ISBN 1-58685-853-X
  1. Architecture, Domestic—United States. 2. Arts and crafts
movement—Influence. 3. Interior decoration—United States. 4.
Dwellings—Remodeling—United States. I. Svendsen, Linda. II. Title.

NA7571.D76 2006
728'.370973—dc22

                                2005027273

■ CONTENTS

▣ PREFACE

Lessons of Old vs. New Arts & Crafts Homes

This book's title, *Along Bungalow Lines,* resurrects a phrase often heard during the early twentieth century, recalling the sweeping popularity that America's bungalow homes enjoyed during their heyday. The phrase was a convenient way to describe other newly built homes whose outward or inward appearance sported some of the typical forms or features associated with bungalows, but didn't necessarily fit into the "true" bungalow mold. For example, when a home was described as built "along bungalow lines," it referred to homes that were either larger in size or different in their planning format than a typical bungalow. Most often used as a real estate sales pitch, the phrase is a not-so-subtle attempt to forge a tangible connection with these other homes to the most popular and modern house in America at that time.

Whether or not today's owners of Arts and Crafts homes can claim much historic perspective on that period, most share an interest in upgrading their vintage nests with at least some of the latest amenities of domestic technology. Fortunately, ever-greater numbers of these homeowners are seeking ways to do so without necessarily sacrificing their home's original charm and character. Prompting this book's title, and also because the subject of bungalows has already been extensively covered elsewhere (including previous books by myself, among others), most of the homes presented here were indeed "built along bungalow lines." With all due respect to the bungalow, it is hoped that the examples seen in this book will encourage a broader interpretation of what may be included in the world of America's Arts and Crafts homes.

A sequel to my previous work, *Beyond the Bungalow: Grand Homes in the Arts & Crafts Tradition* (Gibbs Smith, Publisher, 2005), this book continues the exploration of this less-charted territory of early-twentieth-century houses. In fact, its particular focus was initially planned to be the final segment of the earlier book, until practical limitations (i.e., allotted numbers of pages and images) made all the material difficult to fit in. Thus, a separate book was born, allowing for the images and information to expand accordingly. The distinct departure this book makes from its companion volume is that its primary focus is on vintage Arts and Crafts homes that have been sensitively restored, renovated, or enlarged. It concludes, however, with a diverse selection of newly constructed homes. These show how historic inspiration may be transferred and absorbed into contemporary applications in some innovative ways. In examples throughout the book, the reader will notice that some of these reflect quite literal adaptations of historic precedent, while others show how the design inspiration of Arts and Crafts period homes may also be interpreted more freely. Regardless of one's personal preference for either approach, it is hoped that both will provide the reader with useful design insight along with new ideas to apply to similar situations.

Early-twentieth-century American homes that incorporate the influence of the Arts and Crafts movement are most famously represented by examples of the Craftsman style. The timelessly classic design sensibility of that style provides the predominant thread running through most of this book's examples. However, homes are included to show that American interpretations of the Arts and Crafts influence ranged far beyond the well-defined confines of the Craftsman style. As in *Beyond the Bungalow,* the chapters of this book are arranged to showcase other design influences that "cross-pollinated" the Craftsman style. Some examples also show how a particular style statement made on a home's exterior is not necessarily carried out through its interior. However, most of these homes reflect some elements of the Craftsman taste, and contribute further reinforcement to the common connection of the Arts and Crafts influence that is shared throughout the book. Through learning lessons of the past, the future of Arts and Crafts design will continue to be bright.

—Paul Duchscherer

INTRODUCTION
Bringing the Past into the Present and Future

Historical Overview: Beginnings of the Arts & Crafts Movement

Public interest in the decorative arts and architecture of the Arts and Crafts movement has continued to steadily grow and mature. Longtime devotees have recently observed that today's Arts and Crafts revival has now managed to sustain itself longer than the duration of the original movement. However, to clarify this observation, it should be noted that it makes reference to the movement's primary period of influence in America, not in England where the movement was born.

Although the term *Arts and Crafts* wasn't officially coined in its presently familiar context until the late 1880s, the movement's head start in England had already begun taking shape by the mid-nineteenth century. A watershed event in its early development was the Great Exhibition of 1851 in London, the first of such international extravaganzas that were soon to occur elsewhere across Europe and America. Among the most conspicuous stars of these blockbuster shows were displays of the latest machinery, signaling that modern technology was fast replacing human hands for certain tedious menial tasks. England's distinction at that time as the world's most industrialized nation was soon to be mightily challenged by the rapidly industrializing United States.

Figure 1.

DESIGN FOR A HOUSE (1927).

Presented in Loizeaux's Plan Book No. 7, *this design has many typical Craftsman features. Most striking is the treatment of the lower portions of the chimney and the oversized, trapezoidal brick porch piers, where bricks appear to grow out of irregularly occurring river rock clustered at the foundation. Trios of short, tapering columns support a shallow arch spanning the front porch. One of the roof's clipped (jerkin-headed) gables is oddly skewered by the rising chimney at left. While outwardly resembling a bungalow, by definition, it is not. The home's compact footprint dictated a second floor location for the bathroom and its two bedrooms, one of which is contained in the shed-roof dormer. Upon entry, a staircase rises opposite the front door, and is open to the living room. Adjoining is a first floor den to the right that could have been converted to a third bedroom.*

Figure 2.

HOUSE IN SOUTH PASADENA, CALIFORNIA (c1910).

Sited on a generous corner lot, this shingled and handsomely detailed Craftsman-style home conveys the modest demeanor of a bungalow through its carefully controlled proportions, which belie its larger size. Effective counterpoints to the low sweep of its two forward-facing gables are the tapering forms of irregularly laid river rock and boulder porch columns. A massive matching chimney anchors the overall composition. Fascia boards (bargeboards) are penetrated by square beam ends. The front entry gable's peak is filled with an openwork beam truss inspired by Tudor Revival half-timbering. The color scheme's soft olive green body color and dark umber trim, with terra-cotta accents on the window sash, is in period-appropriate harmony with the neutral stonework.

Figure 3.

GASTON-HOLMAN HOUSE,
PORTLAND, OREGON (1908)

An outstanding Craftsman-style home "built along bungalow lines," this was designed by local architect William Christmas Knighton. Its catslide roof and matching dormer are characterized by their lower eaves' gentle upward sweep. Of deftly crafted proportions, the fully two-and-one-half story house (with an additional full-floor basement) interprets a common overall bungalow form, at an unusually large scale. Set off by newly shingled walls, the only painted exterior elements are the windows, porch railing, and broad curving fascia boards (bargeboards) studded with oversized keyed-tenon details. During a recent major renovation, the undersides of the deep eaves, as well as the numerous large brackets (knee braces), long rafter tails, and squared porch columns, were carefully stripped of all paint. In a subtly elegant effect, their natural wood finish blends well with the shingled walls. Partially enclosed at far left, the front porch has squat columns set on rough, stone-block piers of local volcanic basalt, which is also used to flank the front steps, and around the perimeter foundation. The home's hilltop location has panoramic views over the city, toward the left.

Since cited as fertile breeding grounds of Arts and Crafts sentiments, these world exhibitions unintentionally brought into sharp focus the growing dilemma of "art vs. industry." This conflict of sensibilities could be observed in the declining visibility of products showing traditional skills of handicraft and in a growing emphasis on all things machine-made. Ironically, technology had developed mechanized ways of producing complex ornamental effects that replaced handwork, especially those applied to goods for the home furnishings market. Seizing their moment, most manufacturers were quick to enhance the outward appearance of commonplace products with mechanized applications of gratuitous ornament, intended to impress the customer and sell the product, rather than for any other useful or practical reason. Predictably enough, much of the middle class was dazzled by such low-cost glitz, and the manufacturers were only too happy to give people what they wanted. This runaway situation became one of the core issues of the design reform cause, which would evolve into the Arts and Crafts movement.

Concerns about design reform predated the first Great Exhibition among a few who recognized the darker implications of industrialization. Most important

among these was important architect and designer A. W. N. Pugin (1812–1852), and influential philosopher, art critic, and teacher John Ruskin (1819–1900). Although the personal philosophies of these men differed considerably, both shared a true reverence for the medieval period and its Gothic style, and for the various handcrafted skills embodied in its surviving artifacts and buildings. Each in his way idealized that distant past as a period when the purveyors of traditional craft skills were elevated into professions of high art. They were convinced that a revival of the craft traditions and ideals of the Middle Ages could become working models for muchneeded reforms in the workplace, opening up many new possibilities of more fulfilling and artistic careers for frustrated factory workers with dead-end jobs.

William Morris and His Influence

Among those of England's next generation to pick up the idealistic torch of design reform, the most widely known was William Morris (1834–1896), an avid student of Ruskin. Deeply instilled with a reverence for the lost world of the Middle Ages and its craft traditions, Morris was a visionary and poet, as well as a brilliant pattern designer. His influence colored much of the Gothic-inspired character of design during the first phase of the English Arts and Crafts movement. In 1861, assisted by his charismatic personality and privileged background, Morris galvanized the ener-

gies of some like-minded friends into collaborating on a business venture to produce and sell a range of simple, well designed, handmade goods for the home furnishings market. Distinctly different in appearance from others then available, they offered textiles, wallpaper, ceramic tile, metalwork, art glass, and furniture. Eventually known as Morris and Company, the firm also offered interior design services for clientele who admired their wares.

A primary dilemma that faced Morris and others who later entered into similar handcraft-driven ventures was that the time and cost of design and materials inherent in their products also made them unaffordable for most of the middle class, who were the people who Morris most wanted to reach. Instead, his goods became most fashionable among the affluent intelligentsia. The lofty goal of educating the greater public about the added value of good design, honest construction, and quality materials ultimately had a rather limited effect in England.

As a voice of concern for the dubious fate of factory workers, some factions of the movement found another fervent cause. Morris was among other English Arts and Crafts proponents who also chose to veer into the territory of social reform. They truly believed that by training otherwise disadvantaged factory workers with marketable craft skills, there could be a potential way out for these workers, through their own efforts.

Despite its long evolution and important contributions to both social and design reform, the Arts and Crafts movement was never a truly mainstream influence in either England or America. However, its aesthetic legacy has long since proven to have been an important influence on the subsequent evolution of progressive architecture and decorative arts. In these disciplines, the quest toward ideals of greater simplicity and order helped pave the way for the emerging Modern movement yet to come.

Arts & Crafts in America: Stickley and Hubbard

In America, the Arts and Crafts movement was able to take a faster and stronger foothold than it otherwise might have, largely due to the proselytizing efforts of its early proponents. The most significant and influential of these were Gustav Stickley (1858–1942) and Elbert Hubbard (1856–1915), who each visited England in the 1890s, and came home impressed by what they had observed of the movement's progress and influence. Although each man would develop his own highly personal vision of the movement and the potential for its applications in America, both were also shrewd businessmen. Hubbard and Stickley became concurrently intrigued with the prospects of aligning their commercial business ventures with an idealistic movement imported from England, and promoted their personal ideas with remarkable zeal. These men helped to achieve in America what Morris and his followers were unable to do in England—bring the progressive, reformed aesthetics of the Arts and Crafts movement to the middle class, through relatively affordable handcrafted products of uncommon design integrity—though not quite in the way Morris had envisioned it.

Gustav Stickley came from a large family in Wisconsin and received early training as a stonemason, furniture maker, and metalworker. This background in craft skills added a useful perspective to his particular business success. Several of Stickley's siblings also pursued furniture-making careers, but none

achieved the high profile of Gustav in his prime. In the wake of his 1898 visit to England, Stickley's sense of direction in the furniture business was indelibly altered. While there, he met with prominent Arts and Crafts architects/designers C. F. A. Voysey (1857–1941) and C. R. Ashbee (1863–1942). He also fell under the spell of the work and philosophy of William Morris. Upon returning, he established a furniture workshop in Eastwood, New York, called United Crafts, which he enlarged in 1900 and renamed the Craftsman Workshops. His business soon took off.

Stickley also undertook the publication of his own magazine, *The Craftsman* (1901–1916), which promoted his expanding ventures and became a popular vehicle for spreading the ideals of the Arts and Crafts movement nationwide. He began to market a variety of other home furnishings products that complemented his sturdy slatted furniture, and also produced and published sets of house plans (see Figures 16–17). His magazine's informal mix of editorial coverage effectively showcased his ideas about architecture, decorating, and landscaping, and his personal vision of a complete Craftsman lifestyle. Notably, he was an early proponent of the bungalow as the ideal, simple American home. While Stickley exerted considerable impact on public taste, his success also encouraged other furniture manufacturers to copy (to his financial detriment) the look of his signature Craftsman furniture. By World War I, the popularity of the Craftsman style was already waning. This factor, combined with some ill-advised business decisions, led to his bankruptcy. Once out of the limelight, Stickley retreated to Syracuse, New York, and lived out his life in relative obscurity. An important Arts and Crafts site is Stickley's former home, "Craftsman Farms," in Parsippany, New Jersey. Today it is open to the public as a house museum (see Resources, page 190).

Elbert Hubbard founded the Roycroft community in East Aurora, New York, in 1895, after his 1894 sojourn to England. He had just retired from a successful career as a sales executive with the Larkin Soap Company in nearby Buffalo, and was initially interested in printing and publishing handmade books.

Figure 5.

INTERIOR VIEW OF THE NICOLAI-CAKE-OLSEN HOUSE.

Viewed from the entry vestibule, the living room extends across the front of the house. With most of the other first-floor rooms visible, the compact footprint of the house is apparent. At the bottom of the stairs to the second floor, the landing at center is enclosed by a solid paneled railing wall. The stairs also connect to the kitchen (partially seen beyond). The living room's fireplace is in the corner behind the landing. At left, a nearly room-wide opening fitted with folding french doors leads to the dining room, which is encircled by a bright stenciled frieze that adapts a period design. Off the dining room, a door leads to a small breakfast room that overlooks the rear garden. The warm, vivid hues seen in the Italian Majolica pottery on display throughout this floor inspired the color schemes of the stenciling and the walls. High wainscoting and plate rails of equal height unite both public rooms; in the dining room the inset panels are stained, while the living room's inset panels are painted.

Especially inspired by the Hammersmith Press established by William Morris, Hubbard started out his new venture as the Roycroft Press, but soon it was expanded to include the production of handcrafted furniture, leather goods, and metalwork. Widely known for his humor and wit, Hubbard was prone to sharing his views on many subjects, and became a popular figure on the national lecture circuit. He also proffered his musings in various Roycroft-published books and in his periodicals, including *The Fra* and *The Philistine*. These magazines proved to be useful marketing vehicles for a flourishing mail-order business that purveyed Roycroft-made products across the country. More successful and long-lived than any of the other American crafts communities inspired by English examples, Roycroft at its peak employed over five hundred workers. After Hubbard and his wife, Alice, tragically perished in 1915 with the sinking of the Lusitania, his son Elbert Hubbard II "Bert" assumed leadership of the community. Financial hardships led to its final closure in 1938. Today, the Roycroft community is being revived as a thriving center of America's Arts and Crafts revival, with officially sanctioned "Roycroft Renaissance" artisans working there, and in other parts of the country. Restoration efforts are ongoing for the mostly intact Tudor-inspired buildings of the Roycroft campus, which are a lasting reflection of Hubbard's homage to his English inspiration. First opened in 1905, the now fully restored Roycroft Inn continues to welcome today's Arts and Crafts pilgrims. (See Resources, page 190).

Defining the Bungalow: A Backward Glance

Because it was the most prolific and popular housing phenomenon to sweep early-twentieth-century America, the bungalow's distant ancestry has been well documented in various recent studies. Such interest has helped it to assume its rightful status as a domestic icon in our "housing hall of fame." Despite the high visibility of its rediscovery, there remains for many a sense of confusion as to what officially defines a bungalow. This elusive topic deserves another round of clarification in this book.

Despite the impulse of most people to presume otherwise, dictionaries are not the best places to seek a particularly insightful or comprehensive definition of a bungalow. On this topic, dictionary definitions tend to be quite general, but most do convey the intriguing point that the word was derived from the Hindi *bangala* or *bangla,* referring to either an old Hindu kingdom of India's Bengal region or to that region's indigenous mud-walled dwellings. These houses had high-pitched thatched roofs that extended beyond their walls to form shaded verandas around their perimeters. As part of a bungalow's generic description as being "a one- or one-and-one-half-story" house, most dictionaries also mention a "porch or veranda" as a typical ingredient.

Figure 6.

WENTWORTH HOUSE
PORTLAND, OREGON (1907).

In the historic Irvington district, this house was designed by noted architect Raymond Hockenberry, best known for his design of Oregon's Crater Lake Lodge, and built for Sion R. Wentworth, then-president of the Irvington Tennis Club. Asymmetrically composed, with a slightly flared overhang at the second floor, the two-and-one-half-story shingled design combines Craftsman-style elements with Tudor Revival—inspired half-timbering and diamond-paned sashes on the upper floors and a single hipped-roof dormer and angled bay on the right side. Recent enhancements to the original design include a pergola-topped porte-cochère *(out of view at right) and side gate to the left, which repeat the forms of tapering river rock piers on the entry porch at center. These lend greater balance to the façade's composition. The unusual side gate is made of a solid steel plate pierced with organically curving lines.*

Figure 7.

KIERNAN-LUTZ HOUSE,
SPOKANE, WASHINGTON (1908).

An imposing example of a hipped-roof American foursquare, this home is located in the city's historic South Hill area. Its predominant horizontality and simplicity of forms show influences of both the Craftsman and Prairie styles. The second floor's narrow, horizontal wood siding is more typical of the Colonial Revival style. Two contrasting brick colors were used to create a lively overall pattern and texture for the first-floor walls, and to articulate the outside corners of the square columns on the full-width front porch. Light gray piers supporting the columns and flanking the steps contribute a third brick color. Centered above the front entry, a shallow pediment-like gable also aligns with the attic dormer. Conceived by the current owner, the recently completed paint scheme was inspired by the colors of nature around the house, and complements the brick tones with its subtle palette of a deep warm gray combined with shades of blue-green. The red-orange on the window sash and narrow cream-colored lines under the eaves provide accents.

Because such descriptions avoid any other specific details, one is left wondering if this is simply a reference to the porch or veranda of an Indian *bangala,* or if it is actually meant to refer to the American bungalow. Hopefully, newer dictionary editions will someday clarify this point, and will include more information about regional variations in the use and meaning of the term as well.

The basic common sense that was inherent in the design of the *bangala* was not lost on the British colonists, who admired how the thatched roof overhangs kept most of the hot Indian sun from heating up its mud walls. Creating an ingeniously practical passive cooling system, the form of the building's peaked roof also helped to draw warmer air upward, while also encouraging cooler air to enter at ground level. By the late eighteenth century, the British had already anglicized the word *bangala* into *bungalow,* and had adapted aspects of its basic form to serve as a model for their own dwellings. More refined but still practical, their version of a bungalow was routinely copied far across the British Empire as a basic model for its colonial housing.

Figure 8.

HOUSE IN SAN
FRANCISCO,
CALIFORNIA (1916).

Prominently sited in a hilly urban neighborhood, this gracious home was designed by a local woman architect and builder named Ida McCain. It is is characterized by an extensive use of clinker brick, which faces the entirety of its exterior walls and chimneys. The clinker brick's characteristic irregularity and deeply shaded coloring (the result of deliberate overfiring in the brick kiln) are especially visible in the lower foreground. There, a low garden wall terminates in a prow-like point as it narrows into the front corner of the flatiron-shaped lot. Directly behind the wall, a concrete fountain and curving bench are recently added elements of a redesigned front landscape. Highly visible because of its steep pitch, the red tile roof echoes the brick's reddish tones and is accented by a curving "eyebrow" dormer. Front steps lead up to an enclosed single-story front porch, where an arched iron-and-glass front door is flanked by matching arched niches set with decorative urns. Largely English in its inspiration, this home's formal character is tempered by a Craftsman-style influence seen in its preponderant use of clinker brick.

Eventually, in twentieth-century Britain, inexpensive dwellings also called bungalows were built, often as modest vacation homes. Most of these have little outward distinction other than affordability, and date in the greatest numbers from between the two World Wars. Despite the shared name, they are not at all comparable in terms of planning, features, appearance, or variety to America's bungalows. Typically, these show no outward influence of the Arts and Crafts movement.

The American Bungalow: A Thumbnail Sketch

Written references to bungalows in American publications began to appear in the 1880s in architectural trade journals, and the term was initially applied to examples of rambling seaside vacation homes and modest country houses. Most early examples displayed the stylistic flourishes of the Queen Anne or Shingle styles, and sometimes were a combination of the two. Typically low-slung in proportion, they tended to have a single primary living level, with only secondary sleeping rooms, if any at all, in the attic level. These informal prototypes helped define the characteristic configuration of the American bungalow that was to figure so prominently in middle-class housing only a few years later.

Figure 9 (opposite).

"THE WHITE ROSE" DINING ROOM IN PORTLAND, OREGON (1913; RECENTLY REDECORATED).

In a typical foursquare home in the Rose City, this dining room's basic features are original, but it was recently transformed by an unusual makeover. The owners have a specialized interior design and decorative painting business, and their home showcases examples of their work for prospective clients. An interpretation of British design in the Symbolist tradition of the early twentieth century, this scheme was largely inspired by the work of the famous Scottish architect/designer Charles Rennie Mackintosh (1868–1928). Incorporating metallic silver and gold finishes in its geometric motifs, the hand-painted frieze echoes some aspects of his work and that of his artist wife, Margaret McDonald. Among these is their signature stylized "Glasgow Rose," which repeats in leaded art-glass panels on the sideboard, in handcrafted metalwork on the narrow inscribed panel above it, and on wall sconces. Simpler metalwork accents occur on applied flat ceiling moldings. The inset wainscot panels were given a shaded painted finish, and to further unify the scheme, all of the room's woodwork was ebonized (finished in black). The table's painted top pays homage to the work of Austrian artist Gustave Klimt (1862–1918), a member of the progressive early-twentieth-century Vienna Secessionist group of painters and designers, who also admired the Mackintoshs' work.

Figure 10.

HOUSE IN SAN DIEGO, CALIFORNIA (1915).

Designed by architect Edward Quayle, this shingled South Park area home was recently subject to a major renovation. A later enclosure of the open balcony was removed, which allows the original form of the house to once again be seen. Because the design of the original balcony railing was lost and undocumented, the owners opted for one with cutout designs in its horizontal boards that adapts the "cloud lift" motif associated with the work of Greene & Greene. Unusual on a Craftsman-style house, the boldly arched first-floor openings are original features. Also part of this renovation was a redesign of the front landscape, which added the river rock and brick elements, and the small pergola.

The peak of the bungalow's popularity in America occurred between 1900 and 1930. Certainly there were qualifying examples built a few years before and after those dates, but if a home's construction date is more than ten years out of this period, it likely would have been assigned another name when first built. Before 1900, smaller-scale Victorian-era homes were commonly called cottages. After 1930, when the cachet of the bungalow was diminished by shifting domestic fashions, the earlier term (cottage) regained its popularity for smaller houses. "Cape Cod," another familiar name, was assigned specifically to compact, formulaic one-and-one-half-story Colonial Revival–inspired homes that were especially popular across the country. Dominating much of the post–World War II housing market, the "ranch house," known for its informal open plans and common application to middle-class homes, seems to suggest the most direct planning lineage to our vintage bungalows.

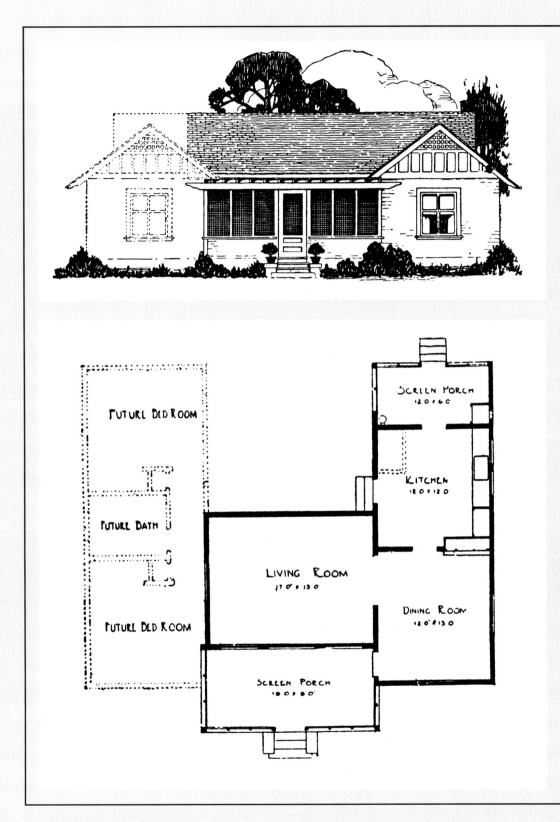

Figure 11.

DESIGN FOR A HOUSE AND ITS FUTURE EXPANSION (1923).

Appearing in The Home, *an annual supplement to* Women's Weekly, *this bungalow design was part of an article about so-called "unit plan" homes, designed to be built in successive phases (units) to accommodate the needs of growing families. This particular design premise was limited by the fact that it needed a larger-than-usual lot to accommodate the outward expansion. Typical lots were too narrow for such a "build-as-you-go" approach. The article made the point that unit plan houses were a good alternative for many families who otherwise "go on paying large sums for rent, because they do not feel justified in spending their resources for a house that will always be inadequate, and cannot afford at present to build the home they need."*

Figure 12.

FLOOR PLAN OF THE HOUSE IN FIGURE 11.

In this proposed layout, the darkened wall outlines indicate the three primary rooms to be built first. Also part of the initial construction phase was the front "screen porch" and another smaller utility porch behind the kitchen. On the left side, the walls with dotted outlines show how two bedrooms and a bathroom could be added later. An enclosed corner pantry is also shown as a future kitchen addition. When built out on three sides, the completed U-shaped plan created the added bonus of a sheltered yet open courtyard space. In this plan's first phase, the absence of any indoor bathroom recalls that when many early bungalows were built, especially those used as vacation homes in rural areas, some had to rely on outdoor toilet facilities.

A fundamental point to remember is that a bungalow is not a housing style but a planning format. Outside impressions alone should not be considered a determining factor in deciding whether or not the term *bungalow* may be accurately assigned to any particular house (SEE FIGURE 1). Today, it is most widely accepted that a "true" bungalow may be correctly defined as a house that has most (if not all) of its bedrooms on the same floor as its primary public spaces. This is as specific as a bungalow definition can get, and it rightly separates the issue of the planning format from a home's architectural style. Therefore, if the floor plan of an early twentieth-century house fits this basic description, its planning allows it to be accurately called a bungalow. Adhering to this point is what allows for so many homes of very different styles and shapes (and "crossover" style combinations) to be rightly considered equivalent siblings in the bungalow family.

Although a first-floor location for the bedrooms is technically what defines a "true" bungalow, the term can also be correctly assigned to homes that may have some additional attic-level bedrooms. However, if a house outwardly resembles a bungalow but has only second-floor bedrooms, it would instead be most accurate to describe it as "bungaloid," or built "along bungalow lines."

Concerning the overall size of a bungalow, a standard of measure remains less clearly defined. Most commonly, bungalows encompass an average of 1,200 to 1,500 square feet on a single level. More generously scaled bungalow floor plans did occur, and as long as they retain the planning format of mostly first-floor bedrooms of their smaller counterparts, they are technically entitled to share their name as well (SEE FIGURES 31–36). Many of these oversized bungalows were custom-designed by architects, and required accordingly higher budgets.

Learning Plan Book Lessons

Throughout the early twentieth century, catalogs of house designs (plan books) that offered full sets of construction documents at a low cost, were widely distributed to prospective homeowners and builders alike. Some plan books were published by Sears, Roebuck and Company, which also began to market prefabricated

The most common expansion was to develop a bungalow's unfinished attic space. In some plan book designs, second-floor attic space was shown fully developed into separate rooms.

"kit houses" by 1909. Numerous others followed their lead, but many firms simply sold the plans. The use of plan book designs generally circumvented any architect's involvement with the project, and most companies offered additional in-house design services for customers who required them. Among the most common customizing request was to reverse a published floor plan into a mirror image of the original, usually to improve a design's orientation on the available building lot. Notably, the majority of America's bungalow designs were originally sold as plan book offerings and presented under the company name of their publisher, with the home's original architect or designer routinely left uncredited.

Most commonly, a bungalow floor plan included a living room, dining room, kitchen, small utility porch, two bedrooms, and one bathroom all on one floor. For households that couldn't quite fit into this standard layout, there were other plans to choose from (still comprised of one floor) that included a third bedroom. Single-floor bungalows having more than three bedrooms are uncommon but did occur; many of these were custom-built designs, while others are simply the result of later additions.

In many bungalow plans, at least one of the bedrooms is provided with two entry doors. Typically, one door connects to a hallway adjoining the bathroom, while the other opens into the living room. Depending on how the bedroom was used, one of these doors could remain locked, allowing for more flexible placement of furniture on either side of it. Decorative folding screens were popular ways to conceal unused doors. A bedroom that had a direct connection to a public area was deemed more suitable for uses other than as a sleeping room. In addition to the two standard bedrooms, some plans had more built-in flexibility in the form of a smaller extra room, usually called a den on most period house plans. While dens were sometimes annexed as additional small bedrooms, they also allowed for use as a home office, a library, a music or sewing room, a guest room, or a combination of these. Such simple but thoughtful features expanded the possibilities of how a home could be used. For these reasons, the bungalow earned its reputation for efficiency and practicality within a compact space. Today, this timely planning lesson remains as valid and effective as ever.

Figure 13 (opposite).

HOUSE IN SEATTLE, WASHINGTON (1909, WITH RECENT ADDITIONS).

Difficult to believe now, but when the current owners acquired this Craftsman-style home, it had lost most of its original character to post–World War II–era "remuddlings." However, its generous lot with two street frontages and Ravenna district location considerably enhanced its potential. Over a ten-year period, a complete two-phase makeover occurred. Most outwardly transforming was the first phase, in which a new third floor was added, and all second-floor rooms were renovated. During the second phase, new features included a detached garage/workshop on the rear side and a roomy period-inspired kitchen. The first-floor projects involved restoration of the living room's original stone fireplace, and re-creation of period-style woodwork that included new high wainscoting and box-beamed ceilings in the living and dining rooms. Surrounding foliage helps blend the revamped building into its landscape.

Future Expansion: Another Bungalow Built-In

Of all the touted qualities associated with the bungalow, the ability to adapt to the changing needs of growing families was an integral part of the most thoughtful plans. This meant that as their spatial needs grew, a family could stay put rather than move.

Although some house designs were initially planned for future expansion outward rather than upward (SEE FIGURES 11–12), this option was limited by lot size, which tended to be rather narrow in most bungalow neighborhoods. Outward expansion was most likely to occur on bungalows in more sprawling or rural settings.

The most common expansion was to develop a bungalow's unfinished attic space. In some plan book designs, second-floor attic space was shown fully developed into separate rooms. Prospective homeowners had the choice of having only the first-floor rooms completed, until additional bedrooms were required (SEE FIGURES 14–15). While not all bungalow plans showed how their attic spaces might be subdivided, many anticipated that future expansion by including a full-sized staircase, to be built as part of the home's initial construction. Other plans also anticipated this need, but instead of providing the staircase, they indicated a specific location (such as within a closet space, storage area, or perhaps at one end of a larger room) for its future construction. In each of these situations, the plans would have specified the installation of openable windows in the gable ends, and also in any of the roof's headroom-expanding dormers, to coincide with the configuration of future attic rooms.

Some bungalows were built with low-pitched roofs that rendered their attics relatively useless, except as ventilated crawl space for secondary storage, perhaps accessible by a pull-down ladder. In these homes, upward expansion is a costly consideration, for it would involve extensive structural reframing of the roof. Added to this is the necessity of reengineering the attic's floor joists to fulfill the load requirements of an active living level, according to most current local building codes. Other critical considerations include providing sufficient allowances for stair width and head clearance, as well as adequate space for a staircase run that isn't excessively steep. Unfortunately, the original staircases to the attic levels of some bungalows were constructed only as access to a storage space. Many of these are far too steep and narrow to be safe for an actively inhabited second floor. Their replacement, or the addition of an entirely new staircase, can be both costly and spatially challenging to compact floor plans.

Basements: A Regional Bonus

Full basements were standard features in bungalows built in areas with colder winters. While some could be tapped for additional living space, most basements were at least initially designated as utility areas. Unless a house was built on a sloping site that allowed for a walk-out basement, with good natural lighting and ventilation through some full-sized windows, its basement tended to be an undesirable location for bedrooms or other active living space. A typical full basement contained the laundry facilities and furnace, as well as specialized storage areas used for family staples and supplies. Areas of built-in shelving were provided for home-canned foods, and sometimes bins were provided to hold root vegetables or other food-related items. Today, many of these naturally cool areas have been adapted into expansive wine cellars. In areas with warmer climates, basements tended to be reduced to small cellars, with usually just enough room to accommodate the furnace and possibly a laundry area, but little else. Especially in the far West and deep South, many bungalows and larger homes alike were built without any basement or cellar areas. Often with outside access rather than any interior stairs, some of these homes have a "raised basement" level that may provide a low-ceilinged storage area, but it is not generally usable as living space. Such raised basements were also employed to help keep rising waters at bay in flood-prone regions.

Downward Expansion: Another Frontier

Today, with or without a basement, the subterranean square footage of a home's original footprint may be the only expansion space left to develop. Many communities have legislated strict height limits to prevent inappropriate or unsightly development out of scale and character with intact older neighborhoods,

(continued on page 26)

Figure 14 (opposite).

DESIGN FOR A HOUSE (1926).

Called "The Kilbourne," this Craftsman-style design was presented in a plan book called Honor Bilt Modern Homes *published by Sears, Roebuck and Company. This bungalow was touted as having "five or eight rooms and bath," which meant that if the homeowner preferred, it could be completed one level at a time, in two separate phases. As a "ready-cut" offering, all the preengineered building materials needed to erect the house as illustrated were provided, from the structural framing to the finish carpentry. For only the five first-floor rooms to be completed, the price was $2,700. To include building out the three planned attic-level rooms at the same time, it cost an additional $300. The simple design is mostly distinguished by its projecting front porch, which creates the impression of an L-shape out of an otherwise rectangular house. The lowered eaves of the porch gable's roof highlight the point of entry, framed by tapering piers and hefty square columns. An attic dormer echoes the form and detailing of the porch gable.*

Figure 15.

FLOOR PLANS FOR THE HOUSE IN FIGURE 14.

The layout of the first floor of "The Kilbourne" is a model of efficiency, and the sizes of the various rooms reflect the typical spatial priorities of bungalow planning. In this characteristic plan, entry is directly into the living room, which opens to the dining room through french doors. However, note the absence of built-ins; by this time, elimination of once-common bungalow features like pocket doors and various built-in furniture helped sustain affordability. However, by the 1920s, there was also a growing fashion for freestanding sets (suites) of matching furniture. For a sense of scale, some furniture items are indicated on this plan; a radio cabinet—a sign of the times—appears on one side of the fireplace, where a built-in bench or bookcase would have once been considered a standard item. Three more rooms (two interconnected) and storage space are added by the attic plan.

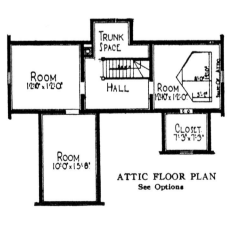

Room
12'-0" x 12'-0"

TRUNK
SPACE

Hall

Room
12'-0" x 12'-0"

ALCOVE OR ATTIC

Room
10'-0" x 15'-8"

Closet
7'-3" x 7'-3"

ATTIC FLOOR PLAN
See Options

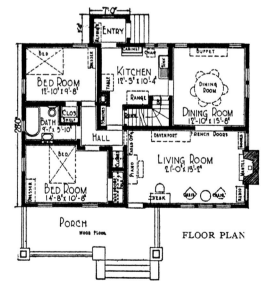

7'-0"

ENTRY

BED
ROOM

CABINET

BUFFET

BED ROOM
12'-10" x 9'-8"

KITCHEN
12'-3" x 10'-4"

DINING
ROOM

RANGE

DINING ROOM
12'-10" x 13'-8"

BATH
9'-1" x 5'-10"

CLOS
SHELF

FRENCH DOORS

HALL

DAVENPORT

28'-0"

BED ROOM
14'-8" x 10'-6"

PIANO

LIVING ROOM
21'-0" x 13'-2"

DESK

MANTEL

PORCH
WOOD FLOOR

FLOOR PLAN

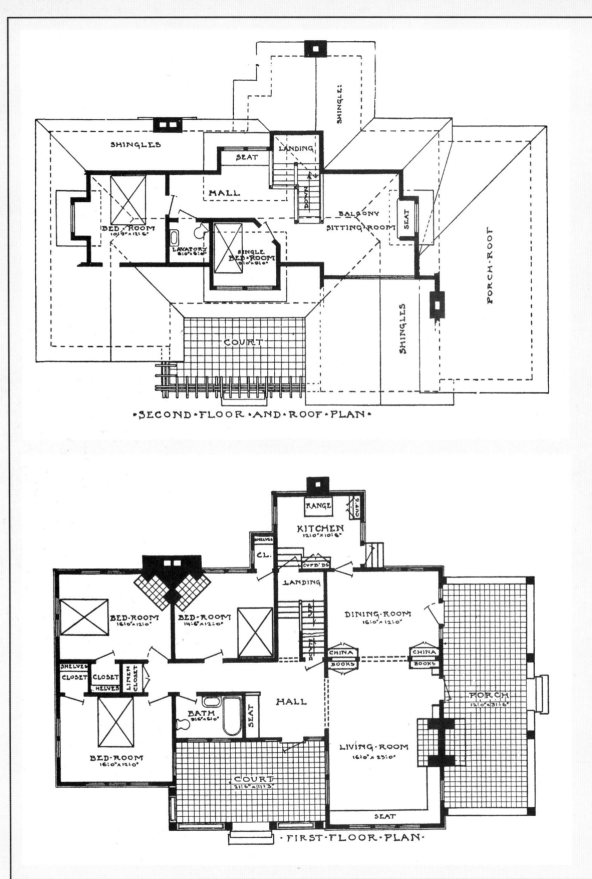

·SECOND·FLOOR·AND·ROOF·PLAN·

·FIRST·FLOOR·PLAN·

Figure 16 (opposite).

DESIGN FOR A HOUSE (1907).

When published by Gustav Stickley in The Craftsman, *the accompanying article stated that this drawing and the plans in Figure 17 were adapted from sketches made by a subscriber, retired architect George D. Rand of Auburndale, Massachusetts. Rand had already built his house in the New Hampshire mountains, in a lakeside setting supposedly similar to this. The article stated that "Mr. Rand kindly gave us permission to use the idea as outlined by him, with such alterations as seemed best to us." The changes remain unspecified, but this resulting design warranted a four-page spread with two additional drawings of interior views. Note that Stickley's logo appears at lower left in the form of a joiner's compass, with his adopted motto "Als ik kan" (If I can) seen within its curving top. Compare this house to the one seen in Figure 18.*

Figure 17.

FLOOR PLANS FOR THE HOUSE IN FIGURE 16.

When viewed in plan, the unequal depth of the projecting front "wings" is apparent. These define an entry court, partially enclosed in front by a low stone wall, which has attached columns supporting the pergola above (compare both floor plans). Inside, the entry hall has a built-in seat, and the wall at right is mostly open to the living room. Opposite the front door, the staircase is through an open doorway; next to it, a door opens to the basement stairs. From its landing, the staircase also connects to the rear kitchen. A short hallway to the left leads to a bathroom and three good-sized bedrooms; two have corner fireplaces that share a chimney. While not entirely clear from looking at the plan, the living room has a vaulted (peaked) two-story ceiling, allowing for a second-floor "balcony sitting room" (directly above the dining room) that overlooks the living room. Partial-height built-in cabinetry separates the dining room from the living room. Adjacent to the two-sided fireplace, a built-in seat wraps around the living room's front end. Doors connect both living and dining room to the large open porch on the right side, which nearly doubles their usable space in good weather. Upstairs, a hall is open to the balcony sitting room, and also adjoins two bedrooms and a half bath.

(continued from page 22)
especially if they are a designated historic district. Such restrictions may eliminate the potential of any upward expansion that would raise the roof, so despite a homeowner's fondest wishes, unless their attic was originally planned and proportioned to be built out as future living space, it may have to remain undeveloped. Faced with such limitations yet wishing to add more living space without any upward or outward additions, some homeowners have opted to explore and exploit their basement-level potential instead.

The downward expansion option may also be considered by those whose home already has a developed attic level or even a full second floor; it tends to avoid many of the inevitable issues and restrictions inherent in undertaking other expansions. Basement-level expansion, fully contained within existing walls (the original footprint), is one of the most minimally intrusive renovation paths. As long as all local building permit and code requirements are met, such an inconspicuous change for any historic house is also less likely to generate local controversy or official resistance, which can create costly delays or perhaps completely derail a worthy project.

Kitchens and Bathrooms: The Great Debate

In most old house remodeling projects, discussion will eventually converge on the subject of what particular design approach should be applied to the bathroom and kitchen areas. In the broadest sense, there are two choices to consider in this regard.

The first approach is also the most conservative one, and remains the overwhelming choice of preservationists and old-house purists everywhere. It is to restore to the maximum extent possible the existing kitchen or bathroom to its original condition. This process includes replicating the cabinetry, fixture style and layout, as well as recreating the rooms' original materials and finishes. Short of having intact originals to work with, this process would be greatly assisted by historic documentation (i.e., original plans or period photographs). Sometimes on close inspection, fragments of original material, or the faint "phantom" outlines of missing features, may still be detectable.

When using the first approach, if a full restoration is desired but no vestiges of the original kitchen or bathroom are to be found, it is still possible to achieve a period-accurate result. This is done by first researching as many period examples of kitchens and bathrooms as possible, from homes of a similar date, scale, and style. While most readily done by consulting information and photographs in various books and periodicals, it is also advisable to visit similar historic homes that have these areas still intact, and to closely observe them. Learning from these examples, it will be possible to create a historically accurate interpretation of the original rooms' appearances. If

starting completely from scratch, however, great care must be taken to ensure the plausible authenticity of the room layouts, window openings, cabinetry features, lighting and plumbing fixtures, wall and ceiling finish materials, and color schemes.

The second design approach that may be applied to kitchens and bathrooms is a far more open-ended proposition. Many people today have chosen to faithfully restore the original condition of their Arts and Crafts home's public rooms, but some draw the line when it comes to kitchen and bathroom design. Their choice is instead to create a contemporary interpretation of a period-inspired kitchen or bathroom design, that successfully adapts the home's vintage sensibility and atmosphere. While some period-appropriate finishes and fixtures may be prominent elements, rooms using this approach are not designed to suggest they are actual period originals. Such designs, at their best, can do an admirable job of harmonizing quite seamlessly with the character and physical fabric of the historic house around them, even if that is all quite original.

Renovation vs. Restoration: A Draw?

In considering these issues regarding kitchens and bathrooms, or of any other areas of old houses, there is no simple answer as to which approach is the best. Each historic house and each homeowner represents a different and unique situation. However, some useful guidance may be found in keeping this thought in mind: one's available budget should not be the only factor in sealing the aesthetic fate of an old house. If homeowners know exactly what they want but simply can't afford to have it right now, they should hold out for the best. In the meantime, temporary interim solutions can surely suffice (SEE FIGURE 29); ultimately, the unwavering goal should be to always respect the historic architectural character and integrity of the house and proceed accordingly. After all, old houses are patient, and won't mind waiting a little longer.

FIGURE 18.

HOUSE IN PORTLAND, OREGON (C1910).

Built for Lewis T. Gilliland, this home in the historic Irvington district appears to be a close adaptation of one that was published in The Craftsman *magazine (see Figures 16 and 17), although the local architect of record is documented as Ellis Lawrence. While not known to be the case with this particular example, the published exterior designs and floor plan arrangements of many Stickley homes, as well as others in countless plan books, were routinely copied or adapted by others (who then often took credit for the design). A comparison of this exterior with Figure 16 will confirm it as nearly a line-for-line duplicate. One noticeable difference: there are groupings of three uniform-height windows in the upper gables, while Stickley's design has a taller window in the center of each grouping. This site, a corner lot in a leafy urban neighborhood, is in sharp contrast to the rolling, bucolic lakeside surroundings depicted in Stickley's illustration.*

Figure 19.

HOUSE IN SANTA BARBARA, CALIFORNIA (C1910; WITH RECENT ADDITIONS).

Perched in the city's Riviera district with an ocean view, this home was occupied by its current owner for many years prior to its recent remodeling. To allow for a new master bedroom suite, a partial second floor was added (only low attic storage space existed), raising the home's original roofline. Designed in context with the original Craftsman style, the new gabled addition repeats the basic form and detailing of an original first-floor front gable at left. The front door, originally on the left side of the wide living room window, was relocated. It now aligns with a new smaller third gable at center, that was added to shelter the top of the new front stairs. Outdoor living areas now include an open terrace under the living room window and a large covered front porch, whose roof supports a deck for the master bedroom. Also added was the single garage at right to match an original one on the left side. All new masonry is of the same pale local sandstone used earlier. New Craftsman-style brackets and wood trim were added as required. On the front stair, porch, and balcony railings, an interpretation of the cloud-lift motif adapts a detail associated with the work of Greene & Greene.

In the Craftsman Taste

Inspiration of the Period's Classic Style

Craftsman Style: A Basic Background

OF ALL the American domestic architectural styles of the early twentieth century, the Craftsman style is what most exemplifies the aesthetic sensibilities of the Arts and Crafts movement. In fact, the current Arts and Crafts revival is being largely advanced by the public's active, growing interest in Craftsman-style architecture and interior design, rather than by a specific rediscovery of the Arts and Crafts movement. Whether in remodeling an existing home or building in entirely new construction, the term "Craftsman Revival" (or sometimes "Neo-Craftsman") seems to be growing in popular usage and application.

The Craftsman style was a cornerstone of the Arts and Crafts influence in America, and was the first housing style to give it tangible form. The use of the term *Craftsman* is strictly an American phenomenon. It originated in 1900 as the brand name that Gustav Stickley assigned his furniture business, Craftsman Workshops. Within a year, he also applied it to his magazine, *The Craftsman,* which he published from 1901 to 1916. During these years, "Craftsman" became a label for almost everything Stickley promoted and sold, including textiles and metalwork

Figure 20.

HOUSE IN SANTA BARBARA, CALIFORNIA (C1910).

Behind a tangle of morning glories, this home's garden setting and recumbent posture exudes a relaxed aura. Its overall form shows a variation of a so-called "airplane bungalow," a term generally assigned to low-slung Craftsman-style homes, with sweepingly wide gables (wings), above which a single second-floor room rises above it all (cockpit). Likely to catch cooling breezes, these aeries made ideal sleeping porches and sometimes were alternately used as game rooms or children's playrooms. This home makes use of natural wood, and its deep eaves, extended rafter tails, and exposed structural timber detailing around the front porch are textbook Craftsman attributes. Horizontal boards on the porch railings have the curving cloud-lift motif favored by Greene & Greene.

Figure 21.

House in Los Angeles, California (c1910).

The boldness of a forward-facing upper gable with robustly scaled brackets and beamwork in this historic West Adams district home lends it an assertive stance recalling the Swiss Chalet style. The home's detailing and crossing-gable form (apparent on the right) are in the Craftsman-style mode. With its variety of brick differing from that of the first floor's walls, square front porch columns, and trapezoidal piers, the large chimney is likely a replacement. Projecting in a grounding gesture, the front porch echoes the main gable. Its right half shelters an elegant wood-and-glass front door and sidelights, while on the left side it extends as outdoor living space. The earthy paint colors are style-sensitive choices.

that complemented his line of sturdy furniture. It also gained prominence as the term describing house plan designs that Stickley both sanctioned and marketed. In the years following Stickley's bankruptcy, his brand name evolved into generic use, but the Craftsman legacy will forever be traceable and indebted to Gustav Stickley, and his once ambitious vision.

At the beginning of the twentieth century, Craftsman was widely perceived as a modern and progressive style, second in this regard only to the Prairie style; at the time, architecture and interior design were in transition from the Victorian era's excesses. Because the bungalow emerged concurrently, many were first built in the Craftsman style. This association stuck in many people's minds and continues today. Despite the fact that bungalow planning was successfully applied to a wide variety of other housing styles, Craftsman remains the most definitive and classic bungalow style of them all.

Forging an Arts and Crafts Connection

While other styles can claim Arts and Crafts influence, none have the significance of the Craftsman style's close relationship to the movement in America. Rather than by any independent link to the movement, most other styles earned their connection by way of some Craftsman influence. Only the English-derived crossovers, like Tudor Revival and English Cottage styles, can claim "direct" connection to the movement. Even so, this is only qualified by their British origins, and only when considering these styles' historical associations with the medieval period, whose craft traditions so resonated with the movement's English founders.

In American renditions of the English styles, associations with their historic sources were indirect, and their links to distant origins of the Arts and Crafts movement were not widely perceived at the

> While other styles can claim Arts and Crafts influence, none have the significance of the Craftsman style's close relationship to the movement in America.

time. In early-twentieth-century America, most housing styles were simply perceived as various available choices to consider; some just happened to be historic revival styles. Then, the emergence, popularity, and decline of any housing style in America (including Craftsman) was determined by the shifting whims of fashion and public taste, not by any links to a progressive design philosophy.

From Arts and Crafts to Craftsman Style

To grasp the essential nature of the Craftsman style, some of the most obvious clues show up in the numerous parallels it shares with the aesthetic tenets of England's original Arts and Crafts movement. After all, these were the providential influences that Stickley and other influential American proponents (particularly Elbert Hubbard of the Roycrofters) had absorbed from their personal experiences in England. There, both Stickley and Hubbard found that among the movement's most basic design tenets was a reverence for natural materials used honestly and simply.

Whether involving considerations of outward form, choice of materials, method of manufacture, or the skill level necessary for production, every aspect of the design process was profoundly affected by making the Arts and Crafts commitment a priority. Design reform was a thoughtful process, geared toward improvement, and certainly not one of mere novelty or fashion. Another important Arts and Crafts tenet was practicality, which could be applied to aspects of function, form, finish, and appropriateness. While the aspiration to create something beautiful was another tenet, it was not considered a goal worthy in itself. By the movement's standards, real beauty was determined and valued both by the handcrafted way in which something was conceived and created, as well as how useful it actually was. This recalls an oft-quoted adage from William

(continued on page 40)

Figure 22.

HOUSE IN DENVER, COLORADO (C1915).

Raised above the sidewalk level of its busy corner site, this home's recently built, stacked-stone retaining wall creates an effective "pedestal" for the entire building. At the corner, the wall's cut-in configuration allows for a sidewalk-level pocket garden that makes an inviting gesture. Clad in red brick, this Craftsman-style home feels more substantial than most, although the light paint color used in the upper parts of its gables helps show off its large brackets (knee braces), and lends more horizontality. An arching window on the right side lights the main stairwell (see Figure 23). A corner-friendly design device, the wraparound front porch also surrounds two sides of the living room (see Figure 24). Its low gabled roof rests on square brick columns with corbelled tops. Providing the covered porch area with unexpected privacy for an urban front yard setting, its brick railing wall is assisted in this by the home's raised siting and its landscaping.

Figure 23 (above).

ENTRY HALL AND STAIRCASE IN THE DENVER HOUSE.

Finely detailed in the Arts and Crafts taste, the main staircase opposite the front door makes a graciously welcoming statement. Along with the other woodwork elements in this room, it is made entirely of quartersawn oak, which is well displayed in the tall newel post. Detailed with chamfered corners, its simple design is repeated at each turn of the rising stair, and includes an integral art-glass light fixture at a midpoint landing. Adding interest with a sense of rhythm, the railing's unusual spindle design has elongated keyhole-shaped cutouts. A display platform and closet at right are built into spaces created by the stair's structure. Both the living and dining room directly adjoin this space from the left. The partly visible doorway leads to a den and a breakfast room connecting to the kitchen.

Figure 24 (opposite).

LIVING ROOM IN THE DENVER HOUSE.

With a favorite motto inscribed above them, the french doors at the far end of this living room are aligned with the front steps, although this home's formal front door is close by (to the left, at one end of the L-shaped front porch). One of the porch columns, with its corbelled brick detailing at the top, is visible outside. During warmer weather, the open french doors promote an easy flow between the house and front porch area. The living room's mahogany woodwork departs from the oak used in the entry hall, and a grid of crossing box beams divides the ceiling. The original fireplace mantel frames an oversized surround of matte-glazed ceramic tile. Softly mottled, with blended shades of gold tinged with blue-green, the tiles recall finishes on art pottery. A pair of recently stenciled, stylized floral elements serve as subtle accents above the mantel. Furnished with mostly Arts and Crafts period pieces, the room is lit and ventilated by either french doors or windows on three sides.

Figure 25 (opposite).

HOUSE IN OAKLAND, CALIFORNIA (C1915).

Filling out most of the width of its lot, this two-story home is separated from its neighbors only by drive-ways. With an original stuccoed exterior, its design interprets the Craftsman style in its gables, with large brackets (knee braces) supporting their eaves, and a trace of Tudor Revival-inspired half-timbering in their peaks. To claim it as private garden space, the owners recently enclosed about half of the front yard with a high wood fence, while the remaining half was relandscaped to soften its effect. The existing front walk and steps were retained, and a central entry gate topped by a pergola-style arbor was added, making a new focal point. To preserve an inviting feeling from the street, wide gaps were left between the fence boards; rectangular cutouts made near the top of each board add a simple detail in the Craftsman mode. The sleeping porch seen in Figure 30 includes the arched window at upper right.

Figure 26 (above).

LIVING ROOM (TOWARDS DINING ROOM) IN THE OAKLAND HOUSE.

A good example of an interior built "along bungalow lines," this home's pairing of living and dining rooms recalls many bungalows. The fireplace surround was recently faced with newly handcrafted, matte-glazed ceramic tile. In the dining room, a large built-in sideboard set into an arch-topped alcove is cantilevered off the side of the house to save floor space. A true "colonnade," almost still intact, once divided these two rooms. On top of the inside end of each of the cabinets and on the underside of the beam directly above, faintly visible "phantom" lines are detectable in the wood finish, which pinpoint where short, tapering columns originally stood. Because matching pilasters (one is visible) are still in place, the precise proportions of the missing columns can be adapted from these. The angled front bay of the living room, visible in Figure 25, is out of view to the left. Paint colors were chosen to flatter the new fireplace tiles and the woodwork.

Figure 27.

SLEEPING PORCH
IN THE OAKLAND HOUSE.

Originally a sleeping porch, this wood-lined room made an ideal conversion to a child's bedroom; it could also function as a guest room or home office. Because it was their original purpose to be used with the windows open more often than not, the walls and ceilings of sleeping porches were given weather-resistant finishes like those used in covered but otherwise outdoor spaces, such as a front porch. The feeling of this compact space is greatly expanded by its large arching windows on two sides (the one at right is seen in Figure 25). Obscured glass was recently installed in the windowpanes to the left to mask an undesirable side outlook.

Figure 28.

DETAIL OF STAIR HALL
IN THE OAKLAND HOUSE.

The once-dingy stair hall was brightened with a soft new paint color and a simple carpet runner, which helps set off the woodwork of the original stair railing. The slats' distinctive spade-shaped cutouts, with long tails on each, adapt an English Arts and Crafts motif. The curtains reproduce a period pattern once sold by Gustav Stickley. To screen off an unsightly view, the window sash of the stair landing windows was fitted with panels of a pale gold and cream-colored slag glass (the type most commonly found in many Arts and Crafts lighting fixtures), obtained from a stained-glass supply shop.

Figure 29 (opposite).

KITCHEN IN THE OAKLAND HOUSE.

Although some practical upgrades were necessary (such as adding the dishwasher), preserving the feeling of an intact period kitchen was the goal of this renovation. Done on a rather limited budget, it is admittedly not the final solution the owners most desired, yet it was what they could afford. Their efforts show how charming and period-appropriate such an "interim" kitchen remodel can be; for some, this may be the final solution. Saving a major sum, the surviving original cabinets were repaired and repainted (most are out of view at right). The former sink wasn't the right period and had to go, and the huge vintage cast-iron sink with integral drain boards was a salvage find that was reconditioned. Its skirt conceals storage space fitted with inexpensive drawer units and wire bins. Period-style pendant lights were added above, an Art Deco glass shade was used on the center light, and the vintage stove was restored. Subtle two-tone paint colors complete the look.

(continued from page 33)
Morris: "Have nothing in your houses that you do not know to be useful, and believe to be beautiful." This standard was routinely applied to architecture, interiors, and decorative arts alike.

In its historical heyday, the Craftsman style managed to resonate with many who were not particularly drawn to, inspired by, or at all familiar with the Arts and Crafts movement. Yet even without any understanding of its philosophy, such people still found contentment living in a Craftsman environment. For them, the fact that they simply liked living there was reason enough for doing so, and no further justification was needed. It is interesting to note that much the same situation exists today; the appeal of the Craftsman style seems to strike a universal chord with or without the Arts and Crafts movement's philosophy attached to it.

Craftsman Style Review: Forms and Features

A basic design tenet of America's Craftsman style that relates to the Arts and Crafts movement is the idea of honesty in design. In both furniture and architecture, that translates to the concept of "revealed construction." Elevating the status of a building's otherwise hidden structural elements into important, integral parts of the visual design was central to building in the Craftsman style. This thinking guided the entire approach to the handling of forms, detailing, and ornament. While the honesty of revealed construction was a noble pursuit, it was not always literally interpreted. In fact, in many of America's finest Craftsman homes, elements that appear to be performing a structural function may, in fact, be merely applied as ornament to express the style's sturdy-looking aesthetic. While this is certainly not without irony when considered in the Arts and Crafts context, it is not a reason to necessarily demean or dismiss such examples as dishonest or inferior.

The style also promoted the use of natural materials, which were recommended to be finished so as to allow their inherent beauty to contribute to the overall design. In the ensuing years, many Craftsman homes that began as showcases of such materials (i.e., stained wood shingles or siding, and stone or brick) have since been painted over. In many such cases, complete restoration of a home's original finishes may be unrealistic, and a tastefully chosen paint scheme must suffice. However, for those contemplating new construction in the Craftsman style, the emphasis on use and beauty of natural materials should remain an important consideration to be respected and pursued today.

There is a characteristic range of building materials most commonly used to express the Craftsman style. For finishing outside walls, typical materials include wide, horizontal clapboard siding, vertical board-and-batten siding, wooden shingles, and various types and textures of brick and stone, sometimes used in combination. Some examples used only a single wall-finish material, although it was common for Craftsman

homes, whether small or large, to employ more than one. Generally, this was a design-driven choice, often done to add horizontality to the lines of the house. A typical inclination of the style, this could be done by using different materials to define separate floor levels, or perhaps to accent gables. Often only a home's foundation line was separately expressed to contrast with the upper walls, which lent a grounding effect.

A home's roof configuration expresses the Craftsman style in the most basic way. The vast majority of homes in this style have some variation of a gabled roof. This can be broadly interpreted, but the simplest version is a single-direction peaked roof with a gable at either end. Many Craftsman bungalows share this simplest form, and sport either forward-facing or side-facing gables. The chosen direction of such a roof makes a big difference in how the house is perceived from the street, and can make it appear either smaller or larger. While not a given feature, dormers provide light and headroom on the attic level, and are common components of this roof configuration on homes of all sizes.

While bungalow roofs were subject to broad interpretation and surprising variety for their size, it was the larger Craftsman homes that offered the most opportunity for variations in roof forms. The use of crossing gables could allow for windows in each of four gable ends, and possibly supplant the need for any dormers. Some examples utilized other variations of roof shapes with multiple gables, and were configured to accommodate L-, T-, or U-shaped house plans. Overall roof forms were often echoed by those of attached front porches, which were typical features of most Craftsman-style homes. Sometimes the "shed-roof" form was utilized for attached porches or other appendages to the main house, such as a bay window. A basic secondary roof form of the Craftsman-style vocabulary, the shed type was also the simplest and, therefore, the least expensive to construct.

Another roof-related form, commonly brought into play as part of Craftsman-style designs, is the open-beamed pergola. While generally considered a garden structure comparable to an arbor, pergolas were sometimes attached to the fronts of Craftsman homes (in lieu of a covered porch) to allow more light into the interior. Some homes featured porch designs that were only partly covered, with the remaining portion of the roof detailed as a pergola. As was the case with a roof's rafter tails, the ends of a pergola's horizontal roof beams were often cut into decorative shapes. By nature of their assembly, pergolas are also good examples of revealed construction, a reason for their popularity in this style context. Another reason was for their primary intended use, which was to support climbing vines. Encouraging such vegetation was widely promoted by style proponents such as Gustav Stickley as useful to help blend a house into its garden surroundings.

Craftsman-style roofs usually have fairly deep overhanging eaves. These help to shelter the outer walls, especially their upper areas, from excessive weathering, and the shadows they cast are also an integral part of this style's appearance. Deep eaves

(continued on page 48)

Figure 30.

HOUSE IN PASADENA, CALIFORNIA (1908).

Designed by noted local architect Frederick Louis Roehrig, this Madison Heights area house is a substantial shingled Craftsman-style design with some influence of the Swiss Chalet style, apparent in the symmetrical composition of the façade, with its single forward-facing gable. Recalling the use of central balconies of many Swiss Chalet façades, the middle window on the second floor is given greater emphasis by a large built-in planter box beneath it, and a bracketed shed-roof awning above it. Creating a better spatial flow within, the front door is located a considerable distance down the right side, which places bedrooms across the front, and public rooms across the back that connect to the rear garden. Missing for many years, the entry pergola framing the front walk was recently rebuilt; it was recreated from period photographs that showed the original one still in place.

Figure 31 (above).

LANTERMAN HOUSE ("EL RETIRO"), LA CAÑADA FLINTRIDGE, CALIFORNIA (1914).

Now obscured by the dense mantle of wisteria on its surrounding pergola, this unusually sprawling Craftsman bungalow was built by Los Angeles physician Dr. Roy Lanterman and his wife, Emily, in the scenic La Cañada Valley, near Pasadena. Its innovative construction of reinforced concrete was used for its fire resistance and seismic strength, and much of the interior was finished with concrete floors. The U-shaped plan of the house created a courtyard area at its center, which is glimpsed directly under the tallest central gable in this view. This also marks the location of a spacious second-floor ballroom (see Figure 36). Outdoor living was a rule in this area's mild climate, and the house has few interior hallways. In fact, its primary bedrooms (see Figure 33) are housed in the wing on the left, and these have only outside entrances. However, they are interconnected through adjoining bathrooms. At right, the front of the wing contains the living room, with french doors opening from three sides. The dining room (see Figure 36) is located directly behind it. Restored and preserved, the Lanterman House is open to the public as a house museum (see Resources, page 190).

Figure 32 (right).

REAR VIEW OF THE LANTERMAN HOUSE.

This view shows the extent to which the Lantermans utilized various opportunities to develop outdoor living areas, advantageously positioned around their home for use at different times of the day. On the left, part of the open pergola that also continues around the front side (see Figure 31) is visible. The gable peak above it has stepped windows at one end of the ballroom (see Figure 35). Although the rear of the house is mostly the domain of the kitchen, maid's room, and other service areas, the Lanterman family's breakfast room (see Figure 34) is surrounded by the screen-enclosed porch that dominates this view. Above it, an open-sided but covered deck/sleeping porch adjoins the second-floor ballroom. Out of view is the original garage structure, which now contains the house museum staff office and a visitor's center, with displays that interpret the house and Lanterman family history.

Figure 33 (opposite).

MASTER BEDROOM
IN THE LANTERMAN HOUSE.

At the front end of the bedroom wing (see Figure 31), this room has french doors (like those at left) on every wall except the one on the right. The mirrored door opens to a bathroom that also connects to another bedroom. Simple cream-colored woodwork includes a picture rail aligned with small crowns on each door and window's top, creating a wide frieze above. Skillful painting on the ceiling adapts vine motifs into a central wreath around the light. Matching perimeter borders are accented by vine sprays, partly extending into the frieze area. The wallpaper below reproduces this room's original pattern. The concrete floor continues outside, where a column of the encircling pergola is visible. On the mantel of the small corner fireplace, which was likely intended to burn coal, are period photographs of Dr. Roy and Emily Lanterman. Lacking any interior hallway to the bedrooms, the only direct access to most of them in this wing is by outside entry, or by passing through other bedrooms and bathrooms. This shows how seriously the Lantermans embraced the idea of "indoor-outdoor living" when planning their home.

Figure 34.

BREAKFAST ROOM IN THE LANTERMAN HOUSE.

While restoration at the Lanterman House has been ongoing for well over a decade, the work in the breakfast room was only recently completed. The primary task was uncovering and restoring the room's extraordinary original hand-painted wall murals. Depicted in soft-focus are scenes of a misty wilderness framed by twisting trees. The portion seen in this view is the most extensive mural area, as most of the room's exterior walls are broken up by doors and windows (see Figure 32); french doors also occur on two sides (one set is just to the left, flanked by two double casement windows). A matching border at the ceiling perimeter was also restored. The woodwork, bordered mosaic tile floor, lighting fixture, and wicker furniture are all original to this room.

Figure 35.

BALLROOM DETAIL IN THE LANTERMAN HOUSE.

The ballroom has a luxuriously festive atmosphere, established by its painting scheme. The delicately pale palette and curvilinear floral motifs were inspired by Europe's mid-eighteenth-century Rococo style. Across the ceiling, slim iron bars entwined with their original artificial rose vines tie the side walls together for greater structural stability and seismic strength; no supporting columns interrupt this considerable expanse. Enhanced by puffy clouds painted across its "sky," the ceiling's shallow barrel-vault form (not apparent in this view) makes it feel higher. In one of two side-facing gables, the stepped windows (see Figure 32) and their elegant swags are repeated at the room's opposite end. A locally famous hostess and music patron, Emily Lanterman lavishly entertained guests, staging musical recitals and other large social events in this room. Other than its sleeping porch areas, this is the only second-floor room, which qualifies the house, despite its scale, as a "true" bungalow. Staircase access from the billiard room below is just out of view to the left.

Figure 36 (opposite).

DINING ROOM IN THE LANTERMAN HOUSE.

Evoking the traditional taste then growing in fashion, a set of dining furniture in the eighteenth-century Chippendale style is a typical component of Colonial Revival interiors. Unlike the home's other public areas, this room's creamy white woodwork and its detailing reflect that influence. Original decorative painting includes a frieze of clustered grapes and leaves framed by matching borders; against a similarly mottled background, the ceiling is painted with coordinating corner and border motifs. Lighting fixtures, draperies, and the blue-violet area carpet are also original features. Set within a border of grey and white marble (plain concrete floors occur in this level's other public rooms), the carpet picks up its subtle hue from the painted areas. Through the door in the far corner, a towering fireplace of rough-hewn granite slabs and boulders dominates one end of the Craftsman-style living room at the front of the house (seen in Figure 31 on the right side). The staircase to the ballroom ascends from a billiard room to the right.

Figure 37.

BARTLETT-WEBSTER HOUSE, SAN DIEGO, CALIFORNIA (1910).

In the South Park neighborhood near Balboa Park, this handsome Craftsman-style home was recently restored. It was designed by noted local architect William Hebbard (who for a time was in partnership with Irving Gill, as Hebbard and Gill). The façade's extra width creates an imposing street presence and show Hebbard's skill in turning the inherent limitations of a shallow corner lot into an advantage. The home's sense of scale is further manipulated by the wide horizontal wood siding of the first floor that extends to the second-floor window sills, making the house appear lower and hinting at the Prairie Style. The siding's warm, natural finish lends greater informality and adds rich color and texture. From beneath a central projection of the second floor, a robustly scaled pergola structure advances forward to make the front entry the façade's focal point. A side garden was enclosed by a new painted lattice fence and covered gate; a similar covered gateway (out of view at right) is aligned at the sidewalk with the main entry.

(continued from page 40)
require support, and, most commonly, their rafter tails (structural roof joists) are left exposed. These are a good and usually functional example of the design tenet of "revealed construction" and are perhaps the most common of all Craftsman-style details. Another typical detail of this style is the use of large brackets (knee braces) beneath the roof eaves. Usually placed for their visual impact rather than for any actual structural support they may provide, brackets may appear in pairs or groupings.

Craftsman-style detailing is another category that was broadly interpreted, but several forms emerge as most characteristic. Among these is the trapezoidal (tapering) column shape, which was an especially common solution for wooden porch columns. These occurred in many variations, from tall and thin to short and thick, and were usually mounted on top of a wide, low pier (base) that was sometimes also tapering in form, and perhaps of a contrasting material such as stone or brick. If ideas for new construction or replacements are being sought, the sheer variety of porch column treatment options in the Craftsman style can be overwhelming, but it is fascinating to observe how many different vintage examples were conceived and built.

Window forms comprise another signature detail of the style, and both double-hung (the vertically sliding type) and casements (the outwardly or inwardly swinging type) were the most popular. It was fairly common for examples of both to appear on the same house. Craftsman homes tend to have numerous windows, as good air circulation was a design priority of the period. For example, many fireplaces feature small windows on either side of the fireplace, and it was most desirable for a bedroom to have windows on two sides. Often, windows were used in groupings of two or three.

If the budget could afford it, another Craftsman-style priority was outdoor access beyond just a front and back door. Many homes were designed with extra outside french doors that were most often included in the public rooms, and sometimes in the bedrooms. Promotion of indoor-outdoor living was a concept that stems from the Craftsman style's early exploitation in areas with mild climates, most famously in California. This concept continued to be seen in many later examples built across the country.

Considering the interiors of Craftsman-style homes, perhaps the most definitive feature is the presence of a fireplace, and many larger homes have more than one. Its form and materials varied widely, but many employed the same brick or stone used elsewhere on the building. A favorite Craftsman device for the placement of a fireplace was within an inglenook, a recess or alcove open to a larger room, that typically includes built-in bench seating on either side of the fireplace (SEE FIGURE 119).

Built-in furniture was another characteristic feature of most Craftsman-style homes. Lauded for their space-saving ability in small bungalows, built-ins also routinely appeared in larger homes, whether or not they were needed to save space. The types of built-in furniture most commonly encountered are bookcases, benches and window seats, china cabinets and sideboards (buffets), and smallish drop-front desks. Most common in bungalows, disappearing, folding, or roll-away beds saved space and sometimes supplanted extra bedrooms.

Another defining feature of Craftsman-style interiors is their woodwork. Ceiling beams (usually hollow, nonstructural "box" beams) are among the most common details, and were generally reserved for the public rooms. Coved ceilings (rounded at the upper walls) also appear, sometimes in bedrooms, and often both kinds of ceiling treatments are used in the same house. Wooden wall paneling, such as a high wainscot topped with a plate rail, is a typical treatment for dining rooms that was sometimes extended into adjacent areas. The most common paneling configuration was the board-and-batten style, which alternated wide vertical boards with thin strips of wood overlaid between each one.

Sometimes the recessed panel areas of a wainscot were inset with a contrasting material, such as fabric or wall covering, or perhaps given a painted finish. Such paneling reinforced a room's horizontal proportions and typically extended about two-thirds of the way up the wall. The area above made an ideal place for a wide decorative frieze. As with Craftsman-style exteriors, the natural materials used to express the style on their interiors were often painted over in later years. However,

in most Craftsman homes, natural woodwork was limited to the public rooms, while the woodwork of the remaining utility (kitchen and bathroom) and private areas (bedrooms) was usually painted with a light-colored enamel.

Today, the touted simplicity of the Craftsman style has come full circle. What resonates once again with many people about Arts and Crafts–influenced design is how its simplicity, honesty of form, and use of materials also aligns with function. While this could well apply to much of modern design, it also suggests that the Craftsman style was a forerunner of the Modern movement. Although now correctly perceived as historic, Craftsman stood out among other contemporaneous styles as the most "alive." With its ability to creatively adopt new products and materials as well as to adapt to the requirements of modern day living, it continues to evolve in its current revival.

Figure 38.

HOUSE IN PASADENA, CALIFORNIA (C1910).

This larger-scale Craftsman-style home was designed by local architect Richard Tyler, and was recently subject to a style-sensitive addition of a new library. In this view, it is located in the gabled, single-story projection on the lower left side of the front façade, which was formerly an open terrace adjoining the living room. Adjacent to it is the original covered front porch to the right (an L-shaped space) that continues around the home's far side. The pitch of the main roof and the detailing of its brackets and exposed rafter tails were adapted to suit the new library addition, which blends quite seamlessly into the original architecture. Its proportions were modeled on an original smaller gable that occurs over an angled bay window on the second floor. In its original position on the side, the front door is sheltered by a small covered porch. Recent landscape additions include the stone post and lantern.

Figure 39.

HOUSE IN SAN DIEGO, CALIFORNIA (1915).

With the clean lines of its stuccoed skin, boxed-in eaves, and grouped casement windows, this Mission Hills area home expresses a strong influence of the Prairie style. However, this impression is offset by a Craftsman-style detail: the pairs of square beams that extend at wide intervals beneath the eaves, crossing as pairs at the corners. Therefore, it could be described more aptly as a crossover hybrid in the Prairie/Craftsman style. Mostly affecting the interiors, a major remodel was recently completed by the current owners that included exterior restoration and repainting. A single-story extension to the left was added in the 1920s, and it was detailed to match the original house.

Figure 40.

LIVING ROOM (TOWARDS DINING ROOM) IN THE HOUSE IN FIGURE 39.

Simple geometric forms in the unusual fireplace mantel and flanking windows as well as a strong horizontal emphasis from the wide molding of the upper walls suggest the Prairie influence. During the renovation process, the fireplace surround of matte-finished tiles, with a blended terra-cotta and blue-green glaze, was discovered to be a 1920s replacement of the plainer original. To harmonize with it, a sponged wall finish blends gold tones with traces of the tile colors. In contrast to this room's quartersawn oak, the dining room's woodwork is gumwood. Its bolder grain is evident on the folded-back french door, and on the high wainscot paneling visible through the doorway. Above it, a new wallpaper pattern adapts a vintage design of a landscape frieze. Recently crafted, the mahogany dining set consists of a long table, matching benches, and a pair of chairs that recall the ebony-pegged furniture of Greene & Greene. Mirrored panels are set into a recess above the built-in sideboard.

Figure 41 (opposite).

KITCHEN IN THE HOUSE IN FIGURE 39.

Most of the original configuration of this room had long since vanished, leaving the remnants of a 1960s kitchen remodel in its wake. Somehow, a row of the original painted cabinets had survived (located where the stove is now), and became the working model for the new replacements. Rejecting white and opting for more color, a warm blue-green was chosen for the major areas of the cabinetry. The color's strength helps to unify the room's various finishes of wood and metal. A 1930 Magic Chef six-burner range is recessed into a white-tiled alcove, and topped by a rounded plaster vent hood, a detail adapted from the kitchen of Greene & Greene's Gamble House in Pasadena. Reprising a handy bungalow-era kitchen favorite, a new built-in version of a Hoosier cabinet is in the far corner. To help reduce its mass, the island's design resembles a piece of freestanding furniture. Out of view at far left, a small breakfast area has french doors opening onto the rear terrace area seen in Figure 42.

Figure 42.

REAR TERRACE OF THE HOUSE IN FIGURE 39.

Although the existing backyard area is quite shallow, the portion directly behind the house was enlisted as space for a new terrace. This design fully exploits its spatial and aesthetic potential. Set as close to the property line as possible, enough room was left for a narrow landscaping buffer along a high rear wall. The area's focal point is the fireplace, positioned to be visible from the interior, opposite the kitchen's french doors. Its stucco-faced design integrates two of the area's four Prairie-inspired columns; a high mantel shelf, supported on angled corbels, spans this composition. The corbels and face of the fireplace are embellished with insets of handcrafted ceramic tile, including a pair of large tile panels, all glazed in a subtle matte-finished green. The fireplace and columns support a series of massive overhead beams that are tied into the rear of the house. An overlay of smaller crossbeams completes this inviting outdoor room.

GREENE & GREENE STYLE

The Influential Masters

The Firm's Beginnings

In the American Arts and Crafts movement, the work by the firm of Greene & Greene is among the most significant and celebrated. Their legacy of architecture, interior design, and decorative arts includes what many now consider the finest domestic examples of American Arts and Crafts design created during the early twentieth century. A partnership of brothers Charles Sumner Greene (1868–1957) and Henry Mather Greene (1870–1954), the firm was based in Pasadena, California.

Their work is also among the most thoroughly documented of any architects of their period. This chapter was included in the book primarily to highlight the powerful influence their work continues to exert on new design work today, whether for remodeled vintage homes (see Figures 58–59), or those of new construction

Figure 43.

LUCY E. WHEELER HOUSE,
LOS ANGELES, CALIFORNIA (1905).

In contrast to their most famous projects, this house is testimony to the fact that Greene & Greene could, and sometimes did, apply their talents to smaller projects with more average budgets. This was commissioned by Lucy E. Wheeler, who was a stenographer and notary. The home's modestly sized corner lot in the historic West Adams district dictated a rather compact design, but the site's two street frontages also provided it with higher visibility. Thoughtfully conceived, the home's form and features are straightforward and simply detailed. The budget precluded most of the firm's signature (costly) design elements, such as their fastidiously rounded rafter tails and beam ends or highly refined interior woodwork of premium woods. Perhaps most distinctive are the purposeful lines of the front porch and second-floor balcony, which exude an elegant spareness on par with some of the best Craftsman designs.

Figure 44.

NATHAN BENTZ HOUSE, SANTA BARBARA, CALIFORNIA (1911).

Built at a time when Charles and Henry Greene were dividing their firm's project responsibilities between themselves, the design of this hillside home overlooking the ocean is principally credited to Henry Greene. It was built for Nathan Bentz, whose interest in the Oriental arts extended to his Santa Barbara shop. Nathan's brother John had previously hired Greene & Greene to design a model house in 1906 on Pasadena acreage being developed into residential lots, so within the Bentz family there was already a working familiarity established with the architects. This view shows the rear elevation and how precipitously the land drops away. Angled to capture views, the shingled home's broadly gabled form rests on a projecting lower level of brick, lined with arched openings, with open terraces above. Because more of the building is visible from below, it appears much more imposing than on the uphill side, where a timber bridge to the entry is another artistic concession to this sloping site. While considered the last of the genre of wooden houses for which the Greenes are best known, this project pioneered the firm's use of steel I-beam reinforcement for the structure.

(see Figures 185–190). While necessarily limited to only a few examples of the Greenes' work, those included here were chosen to provide a sense of the architects' range, extending from a modest commission (the Lucy E. Wheeler House [1905], Figure 43), to a medium-sized one (the Nathan Bentz House [1911], Figure 44), to a grandly scaled example (the Henry M. Robinson House [1905–1906], Figures 49–55). A relatively modest project that Henry Greene completed on his own (the Thomas Gould Jr. House (1920–1925), Figures 45–48) shows his later evolution of the firm's signature style.

Prior to their moving to Pasadena in 1893, Charles and Henry studied architecture at the Massachusetts Institute of Technology, and then worked briefly in the Boston area. Familial responsibility as well as business opportunities prompted them to join their parents, who had already relocated to Pasadena because of health concerns, which were alleviated by its mild climate. That city was then in transition from being a seasonal winter resort, popular with eastern and midwestern retirees, to becoming a prestigious residential enclave, attracting some of America's most prominent families. It would be a challenge for the Greenes to cultivate a clientele affluent enough to afford the kind of projects that would establish and sustain the firm's eventual high reputation. In the meantime, they worked on a variety of homes, some surprisingly modest in both scale and budget. Outwardly, some of their early projects reflected the popular taste of the late Victorian era, especially the Queen Anne and Colonial Revival styles. The firm's move toward their signature Arts and Crafts style took several years to develop and mature.

On their way west to Pasadena, the brothers decided to stop in Chicago and visit the 1893 World's Columbian Exposition, whose buildings were a showcase of America's latest architecture and design trends. Dominated by gleaming white edifices conceived in the style of Beaux-Arts classicism, the exposition grounds were popularly nicknamed "The White City." However, the most lasting impression on the brothers was made by an authentically detailed, reduced-scale replica of a Japanese timber-frame shrine on display. Built by master craftsmen from Japan using traditional joinery techniques, this structure was unlike anything the brothers had seen. Both straightforward and elegant, the design sensibility captivated them, and the possibilities inherent in its construction process also intrigued them. Although neither of them would ever travel to Asia, their Chicago visit to the Japanese timber-frame shrine would have a profound effect on their future work.

Building a Legacy

Pasadena remains the mecca for Greene & Greene enthusiasts, and some of their most important commissions survive there. Among these are the Henry M. Robinson House (see Figures 49–55), the Robert R. Blacker House (1907–1909), and the David B. Gamble House (1907–1909). The latter two projects are on a short list of homes euphemistically dubbed the "ultimate bungalows," which represent the firm's finest work produced during the peak years of the brothers' practice together. Other projects of this select group include the Charles M. Pratt House in Ojai, California (1908–1911), and the William R. Thorsen House in Berkeley, California (1908–1910). Today, the firm of Greene & Greene remains most widely known for these examples that interpret a highly personalized vision of the Craftsman style on large, wooden houses.

Figure 45.

THOMAS GOULD JR. HOUSE,
VENTURA, CALIFORNIA (1924).

Around 1911, Mrs. Thomas Gould Jr. first became interested in building a Greene & Greene house. As a subscriber to Gustav Stickley's The Craftsman *magazine, she had admired the published designs of the firm. The Goulds couldn't afford to proceed with a new house until 1920, when they met with Henry Greene to discuss the possibilities of their project. By then, Charles Greene had moved with his family to Carmel, while Henry continued running their Pasadena practice until it was officially reorganized in 1922. In a revealing sign of the times, Henry first proposed working in a Spanish or Mediterranean style, which he felt had an appropriate regional context in Southern California and might be better for resale. But Mrs. Gould's Craftsman preference prevailed. First, Henry sketched out a grander two-story design, but soon after the Goulds bought this rural site overlooking the Pacific, Henry's ideas necessarily took a more modest turn. The final design's form is a long rectangle with a partial second story toward its center. Clad in horizontal wood siding of alternating widths, the home's simplified Craftsman-style details are quietly elegant.*

Of all their projects, the Gamble House remains the most famous and celebrated, due in part to its higher public profile as a house museum that has been open to the public since 1966. At that time, the home's long-term preservation was ensured by the Gamble family's generous gift of their parent's house to the city of Pasadena. A conditional agreement assigned the administrative duties of the house to the School of Architecture at the University of Southern California (USC) in Los Angeles. What makes the Gamble House such a rare study resource is its remarkably intact condition. While routine maintenance has required extensive and costly ongoing attention, the home remains in its original state. Perhaps even more remarkable is the survival of its original interior features as well as its architect-

designed collection of furnishings. An ongoing benefit to visitors and students of architecture alike, the accessibility of the Gamble House has established it as an important center of study concerning the American Arts and Crafts movement, as well as a showcase for the extraordinary design work of two very gifted practitioners.

All of the Greenes' collaborative work was produced over a relatively short period of time. After Charles moved with his family to Carmel in 1916, the firm remained in operation under Henry's direction. It survived (at least in name) until 1922, when it was finally dissolved. Henry reorganized the business under his name only and continued working in Pasadena, never leaving that area. Charles remained in Carmel, where he had built a home and studio. Although he did produce occa-

sional design work, mostly for previous clients, Charles became more engaged with the fine arts rather than architecture in his later years.

The Greene & Greene Style

Even in their more modest projects, the attention to detail and quality of craftsmanship displayed in their homes and interiors is exceptional. With a demanding sense of perfection that bordered on obsession, the Greenes expended much of their time and energy working out design decisions about structural framing, joinery, woodwork, and finishes. For projects with budgets sufficient to include custom-designed and handcrafted furniture, that additional demand pushed their standards even

(continued on page 61)

Figure 46.

ENTRY AND STAIR IN THE GOULD HOUSE.

Starting with the design of the extra-wide front door, with its subtly positioned divided lights, Henry Greene carried the simple, well-crafted quality of the home's exterior to its interior. Entry is directly into the living room, in the bungalow manner, where a staircase rises immediately to the right. Flanked by handcrafted copper sconces on the landing, a tall arching mirror is set into a shallow recess. Below it is a low built-in drawer, with a shallow carved front and unusual recessed pulls. Combined with the stair's wooden screen wall, this grouping of architect-designed features enriches the room's otherwise rather simple detailing. Now considerably faded, the woodwork's original greenish stain is still detectable.

Figure 47.

LIVING ROOM FIREPLACE IN THE GOULD HOUSE.

Plain in overall form except for its tapering chimney, this original fireplace shows the work of Pasadena tilemaker Ernest Batchelder. Characteristic of his work are the distinctive matte-finished glazes, softly shaded colorings, and low-relief accent tiles with pictorial imagery seen here. The popularity of Batchelder's tiles at the time caused his work to be widely copied by others. The fireplace opening is framed by a narrow, rounded-edge border, and flanked by a pair of opposing vertical tile panels depicting tall, stylized fir trees. Set into plain field tiles above are smaller accent tiles with a parrot motif. In lieu of any mantel shelf, a shallow tile crown molding trims out the top of the surround. Visible beyond is a den with a built-in window seat set into an angled bay, which has drawers underneath with similarly handcarved detailing as the one seen on the landing in Figure 46. Note the coordination of simple horizontal linear detailing on the french door and windows.

Figure 48.

DINING ROOM IN THE GOULD HOUSE.

Brightly lit from windows on two sides, this room's design includes a built-in sideboard set into a shallow bay. The leaded art-glass windows above it were originally designed as the doors of a built-in china cabinet that was once the upper part of the existing sideboard. When the china cabinet was removed, the wall space behind it was opened up, and the art-glass panels were adapted as casement windows. Their irregular leaded grids of mostly clear glass incorporate a scattering of art-glass details depicting stylized hummingbirds and floral forms. These occur across the tops of all the panels, and down the length of the narrower ones. Designed by Henry Greene, the art glass is testimony to his skill at conceiving distinctive decorative effects, a talent more usually ascribed to Charles. The ceiling fixture is a later adaptation of the lantern form associated with Greene & Greene's most famous projects. The original wooden drapery hardware survives above the windows.

(continued from page 57)

higher. A flip side of this perfectionism was that, on some occasions, project delays and cost overruns aggravated a few of their clients. However, most understood, anticipated, and eventually reaped the rewards of exercising patience. The Greenes' design work represents the American Arts and Crafts sensibility pushed to its far limits of quality and refinement, and was never exceeded.

While there were significant variations in the outward appearance of the brothers' projects over the full course of their careers, the best-known houses associated with their brief "ultimate bungalow" period share similarities, and display elegant variations of the Craftsman-style sensibility. It was through these projects that the firm's signature style most recognized today was fully developed and codified. Exhibiting a near-consistent use of shingled walls as a unifying feature, the overall forms of these homes are composed with varying degrees of complexity. The siting of each one shows a sensitive and appropriate response to its immediate environment. Roofs with multiple gables of shallow pitch and deep overhanging eaves are a characteristic feature. Along with exposed rafter tails, a detail for which they are particularly noted is their use of so-called "outriggers" (extended and exposed major structural roof beams). Recalling the Arts and Crafts tenet of revealed construction, these project as significant design elements. Another of the firm's signature details is a meticulous rounding off of the squared ends and edges of these beams, as well those of other visible structural elements. This effect was applied in varying degrees to both exterior and interior woodwork.

The Greenes closely considered the relationships between their projects' interior and exterior living spaces. To a large extent, this was a priority, for California's mild climate encouraged year-round outdoor living, and their clients expected to be able to enjoy this luxury on a routine basis. Therefore, generous outdoor porch and terrace areas (both open and covered) were typical features. An example of restraint amid the elegance, the floor finish materials of most outdoor spaces were limited to simple terra-cotta tiles bordered in plain brick. Especially in the firm's larger projects, public rooms are often provided with direct outside access. They also favored the use of open-air sleeping porches, which sometimes (as with the Gamble House)

Figure 49.

HENRY M. ROBINSON HOUSE, PASADENA, CALIFORNIA (1905–1906).

Sited at the edge of the Arroyo Seco, this home is a pivotal link in the evolution of Greene & Greene's most significant phase, which soon yielded their so-called "ultimate bungalows." The centerpiece of a multi-acre estate, this house and its grounds comprise a unique urban oasis. The current owners have meticulously restored the exterior as well as the home's primary public rooms. Some of the secondary interior areas were creatively renovated (see Figures 52–53). They have also commissioned exact reproductions of the original architect-designed furnishings. Quite different in feeling from the wood-intensive style most linked to the Greenes' work, this home's exterior walls are finished with rough-cast stucco. Its soft ochre color harmonizes with the building's other elements and its setting. The angled wing at right contains utility and service areas. The second-floor half-timbering details show some English influence, perhaps inspired by Charles Greene's extended honeymoon trip there in 1901 (his wife was English). Some of the first-floor corners feature battered (sloping) buttresses that recall a design detail of English Arts and Crafts architect/designer C. F. A. Voysey. These and the largest chimney also suggest a possible influence of Native American adobe structures. In the foreground is a new Japanese-style garden, one of several distinctive landscape features recently developed on the sprawling grounds.

Figure 50.

ENTRY HALL
IN THE ROBINSON HOUSE.

When built, this was the most impressive entry hall yet created by Greene & Greene. Directly opposite the front door, the stunning staircase ascends from a broad landing, along a board-and-batten Port Orford cedar—paneled wall. Offset by a series of pegged cross-bars, rhythmically arranged like musical notes, the paneling's vertical boards are of continuous lengths and alternating widths. The stair treads' design resembles a carefully cantilevered sequence of box-like wooden forms. In an elegant design of revealed construction, the stair railing utilizes pegged and through-tenon detailing. Occurring on three sides of the two-story space, the railing seen at the upper right continues the design of the angled stair. Suspended from a decorative wooden backplate on the ceiling is a hexagonal art-glass lantern with an Oriental influence. Art glass also occurs in wall sconces and on the front door (out of view at right). Mostly of plain glass, the unusually wide pocket door to the dining room (at right) is repeated in the living room doorway on the room's opposite end. Brothers John and Peter Hall, master woodworkers from Sweden, firmly established their long working relationship with the architects on this project.

Figure 51.

DEN IN THE
ROBINSON HOUSE.

A cozy retreat convenient to the main living areas, the den has a sitting area centered around its corner brick fireplace. Also a library, the room is lined with built-in bookcases. The original steel fireplace hood with a terra-cotta tile inset remains in place. Reproducing missing original designs are the firebox, and a simple wood mantel supported by chains from wrought-iron straps, which straddle a pair of projecting V-shaped brick ridges that extend to the ceiling. Adjacent walls incorporate the same brick. At right, a high-back built-in bench, with an attached storage cabinet on its rear side, creates a partial inglenook. This built-in also screens the fireplace area from doors leading to the living room and the entry hall (out of view, at right). On the sides of the bench, butterfly key tenons, named for their shape, link adjoining flat boards. A 1920s addition doubled this room's size, extending it more prominently from the front façade (see Figure 49). A large roof deck was created above it, with railings set between the taller, angled corner buttresses. The room's original size was limited to where board-and-batten paneling is used between the beams. A massive crossbeam replaced the room's former end wall. Taller bookcases matching the originals were added around the extended wall areas.

Figure 52.

KITCHEN IN THE
ROBINSON HOUSE.

Sensitively remodeled by the current owners, the kitchen continues to occupy its original location. Fortunately, the vintage curving plaster hood survived intact, so the range (and sink) locations remain unchanged in the new layout. The distinctive cabinets Greene & Greene designed for this area were carefully adapted as models for the new cabinetry, and identical hardware was used. Underneath a band of windows along the left wall, new lower cabinets were added, with marble insets in the wood countertop for rolling out pastry. With considerable storage areas below, a freestanding island (plumbed for an extra sink and a dishwasher) was also added. The island supplants the function of the center worktable of the original kitchen. The pot rack with a central pendant light is suspended from a wooden backplate adapted from one on the entry hall ceiling (see Figure 50). On the right, period-style cabinet door facings conceal new refrigerators, which include drawer-style units below. In the foreground, the counter replaced a wall that originally separated the kitchen from a screened utility porch and the back door. Now divided only by this counter, the old porch area has been absorbed into the new kitchen as the breakfast area, and one of its walls is lined with new matching cabinetry.

Figure 53.

BATHROOM IN THE
ROBINSON HOUSE.

One of the home's recently remodeled bathrooms, this retains its original cast-iron footed tub, which was refinished and refitted with new nickel-plated hardware. A stall shower is out of view to the left. Above the marble-topped double-sink counter, wooden wall sconces adapt a Greene & Greene design. Next to the window, a period chair with a high seat and footrest was designed as a vantage for watching billiard games. The door opening in the foreground was widened to allow for a new sliding door with translucent inset panels, which was modeled after original pocket doors to the dining and living rooms (see Figure 50). Located on the second floor of the service wing above the kitchen, this is part of an area that was originally comprised of a servants' bathroom (now reconfigured as shown) at the end of a hallway that passed by the maids' rooms. In the recent remodel, those smallish rooms were combined into a single larger adjoining space, which now functions as a generous exercise room.

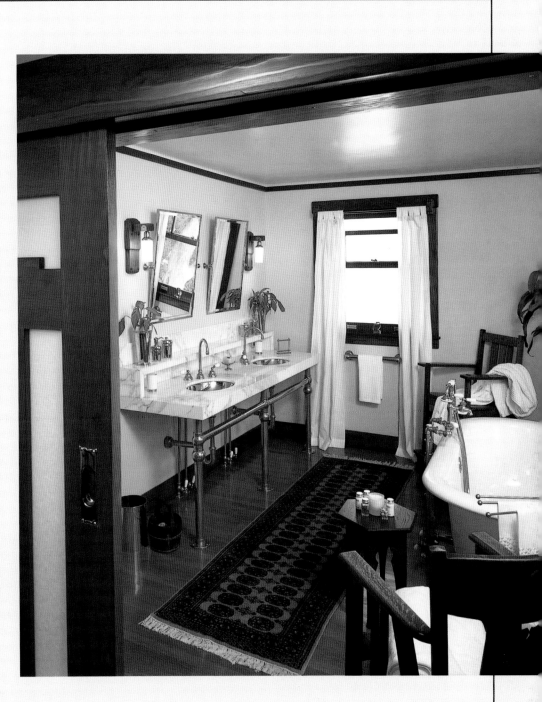

were incorporated as prominent elements of the overall design. Most often these were placed adjacent to family bedrooms for exclusive access. For their interior millwork, with exposed joinery and ebony-pegged details, they favored the finest woods, from Port Orford cedar to teak and mahogany.

Another key aspect in their most important commissions was a prominent use of leaded art glass, which added vivid counterpoints of color and pattern to the highly atmospheric spaces. Most of the glass designs are abstracted representations of natural forms. Some of the Greenes' most significant rooms are completely integrated ensembles of multiple art-glass applications to doors, windows, cabinet doors, and lighting fixtures. Much of the firm's decorative design work, including their art glass and furniture, is attributed specifically to the talents of Charles Greene, but some later projects proved that Henry was also highly talented at such design work (see Figures 46–48).

The Greenes also paid close attention to the service and utility areas of their homes; surviving examples such as the Gamble House show the care taken to ensure high quality in the design of spaces that were mostly used by servants. In their treatment of bathrooms, the Greenes tended to keep their designs simple, and for the most part were driven more by function and practicality than by making a style statement. Most employ unadorned, white tile treatments on floors and walls, with plumbing fixtures that were also found in much less expensive homes. Some do have architect-designed medicine cabinets and lighting fixtures, but these tend to be repeated in a project's multiple bathrooms.

Greene & Greene Influence

The firm's work came to be recognized and admired by other proponents of the American Arts and Crafts movement, including Gustav Stickley, who published numerous examples of it in *The Craftsman* magazine. The Greenes also admired Stickley's work, specifying his furniture designs for some of their projects where lower budgets precluded custom-built furniture designs. They were also acquainted with Frank Lloyd Wright, who respected and admired the high caliber and integrity of their work. Their fame in Arts and Crafts circles extended to England, and the

Figure 54.

SUNROOM DETAIL IN THE ROBINSON HOUSE.

An intimately scaled treasury of Charles Greene's skilled artistry at woodcarving, the wood-paneled sunroom is embellished with low-relief examples of his work. Subtly realized moldings and figural elements occur at the ceiling perimeter, in areas of the frieze, and on the wall panels. Among these are stylized forms symbolizing aspects of nature that range from the sun and moon, to clouds and stars, to ocean and mountains. Added in 1918, this sunroom resulted from the enclosure of an original open pergola that adjoined one end of the living room. At the same time, the space directly above this room was also enclosed, comprising a two-story addition to the house (seen in Figure 49 on the far left side).

Greenes were visited by designer Charles Robert Ashbee (1863–1942), a luminary of the later British Arts and Crafts movement, who founded the Guild of Handicraft in England. An organization of fine craftspeople, Ashbee's venture was a working model for similar craft-producing ventures that occurred elsewhere, including America's Roycroft, Byrdcliffe, Rose Valley, and Arden communities. For a time, Greene & Greene's work took on increasing national prominence from its broad exposure, and became an inspiration to other architects and designers. Some examples of Craftsman-style work created by other architects working at the same time in and around the Pasadena area are occasionally mistaken for the work of Greene & Greene (SEE FIGURES 38 and 56), and such comparisons are usually received as a compliment.

More recently, in the context of the Arts and Crafts revival, Greene & Greene's work has been thoroughly and widely documented by a succession of books, in which the significance of their work has been evaluated, discussed, and reassessed. If anything, all this renewed attention has made the firm's reputation loom larger than ever. As inspiration for new work, the characteristic design repertoire of Greene & Greene has become a goldmine of ideas for many recently conceived remodels and newly-built projects in California, as well as across the country (SEE FIGURES 10, 19, 58, 59, 97, 128, 129, 167, 185–188).

Some argue or dispute the integrity and appropriateness of this phenomenon, objecting to such literal borrowing of their signature design details, especially so far removed from their original context. Yet others embrace the idea of such freely interpreted inspiration, and believe that good ideas simply gain new life when they are artistically reinterpreted elsewhere. Certainly few people today can afford to consider the possibility of acquiring an original Greene & Greene–designed home, especially one of their famous ones. Acquiring original examples of their furniture, art glass, lighting, or other decorative arts is probably even more remote, because most of these things are already in museums or private collections. But still the adulation grows, and today, many homeowners as well as architects, designers, and craftspeople are more than willing to take up the Greene & Greene torch.

Figure 55.

POOL AREA OF THE ROBINSON HOUSE.

This property enjoys views of Pasadena's gracefully arching Colorado Street Bridge (1912–1913), which spans the Arroyo Seco, a wooded creekbed canyon providing undeveloped open space for the area. While handy to the service and utility wing of the house (toward the left), the pool area was landscaped to effectively buffer it from that vantage. Convenient for entertaining, a covered, open-sided pavilion fitted with an outdoor kitchen is partly visible at left. In its form and finish materials, the pool's overall design is restrained and unobtrusive. The pool includes a rectangular spa near the sitting area. From there, it curves out in a broad arc, detailed with a so-called "infinity edge," and seems to float over the Arroyo. Tinted a warm limestone color, the simple concrete paving includes some occasional planting pockets that further soften it. Visible portions of the pool's perimeter and other paved areas have understated brick borders that match other masonry on the property.

Figure 56.

HOUSE IN PASADENA, CALIFORNIA (C1910).

Today, outward similarities to the Greenes' work may lend some credence to speculation about influences observed in the work of other architects practicing at the same time. Prominent Pasadena architect Sylvanus Marston was responsible for the design of this home, which recalls some of the Greenes' work. However, the extent or possibility of their actual influence remains only conjectural. Like the Greenes, Marston also had projects published nationally in books and periodicals, and was in local demand during the Craftsman style's height of popularity. Set far back from the street, this home was recently subject to a major addition (discretely undetectable in this view) on its rear side. Dominated by the broad sweep of a shallow gabled roof, its composition includes a matching but smaller second-floor gable projecting from the left. A wisteria-clad front porch provides anchoring, with a gable almost as wide as the upper roof's, and a concrete floor almost level with the ground. Extending from the side at right are other matching gables. Expressing classic Craftsman details are the long shingles, deep eaves with exposed rafter tails, and protruding structural "outriggers" (roof beams). Part of a recent relandscaping, a naturalistic effect is created by randomly placed boulders and clumps of ornamental grasses set into the lawn, further linking the house to its rolling site. Existing concrete stepping-stones at right, cast to resemble large flagstones, were retained in the new design.

Figure 57 (opposite).

LIVING ROOM (TOWARD DINING ROOM) IN THE HOUSE IN FIGURE 56.

An open colonnade opposite the fireplace divides this living room from the entry hall (out of view), which adjoins a staircase (enclosed on the first floor), a den with built-in bookshelves, and access to rear utility and service areas. Original woodwork in these areas is more conventionally designed compared to that of Greene & Greene—designed homes of this period and scale. Small corbel blocks add interest to the tops of the door and window casings. With a facing of subtly shaded tan brick, the fireplace is simple in its materials, but its stylish "horseshoe arch" opening is a more unusual feature. Most of the Arts and Crafts furnishings and lighting in these rooms are reproductions. The multi-shaded dining room fixture was inspired by a Greene & Greene original. Darkly stained woodwork in the living room contrasts with the dining room's lighter quartersawn oak. Fitted with sets of fold-back french doors, the wide doorway is repeated across the dining room, where it leads to the newly added family room (see Figure 58). Partly seen are single-light french doors to a side terrace and the pool area seen in Figure 59.

Figure 58.

FAMILY ROOM IN THE HOUSE IN FIGURE 56.

Adding considerable space and a long list of other amenities, a major new addition includes this spacious L-shaped family room. A seating area in the foreground was once an open terrace, which later had been inappropriately enclosed as a sunroom that adjoined the dining room. The current owners wanted a bright, airy, and informal living area that improved the home's indoor-outdoor relationship. For design continuity, details from original areas were repeated in the woodwork of the door- and window- casing corbels, as well as in the box beams. The ceiling beam layout was necessarily guided by the placement and visibility of new structural beams that were required support for the two-story addition. Greene & Greene's design sensibility was the style inspiration for the linear divisions above the fireplace, which also includes recessed built-in cabinets above and below the thick mantel shelf. French doors at right open to a raised rear terrace, which widens as it wraps around the new addition toward the left (see Figure 59). A corner window grouping overlooks the new pool and spa area. Besides added bedroom space above, the addition also contains an expanded open kitchen and breakfast area toward the right, along with other new service and storage areas that are oriented toward a side entrance adjacent to a side driveway and the garage.

Figure 59.

REAR ADDITION AND POOL AREA OF THE HOUSE IN FIGURE 56.

A key element that especially informed the design of the new addition was the home's original gables. These were a useful device in resolving issues raised in expanding the interior volume, and in extending the existing roofline. Also marking the point on the side from which the existing structure was expanded toward the rear, one of the home's original signature gables shades a two-story rounded bay at far right. Except for that and a detached garage at far left, only new construction is visible in this view. The gables' forms are brought into play closer to the ground by a pergola structure, employed on two sides of the addition, that shelters raised terrace areas. Similarly-shaped gables occur in its substantial yet open structural framing. Narrow strips of wood across its top provide filtered shade. Softened by plantings, textural interest is added by the new clinker brick and flagstone paving. Stacked stone is used on a low wall and stairs that leads to an open lawn area to the left. A spa with a waterfall (out of view) is attached to the pool on the far right. Wrought-iron railings adapt a period metalwork design by Greene & Greene.

■

PRAIRIE EVOLUTION
Progressive Period-Style Influence

Prairie Style Background

To put this early-twentieth-century style into its historic perspective, it is useful to understand the significance of the name *Prairie* (French for "extensive meadow"). It was so named for the style's inspiration from the ever-present horizontal line of midwestern America's open prairie landscape. Emerging about the same time as Craftsman, the Prairie style was also widely perceived as new and modern, but its basis was far more abstract. Instead of any preoccupation with exposed structural elements, it was primarily expressed as an interplay of spatial volumes arranged into building compositions with insistently horizontal lines. Unlike Craftsman, it relied on overall impression, and downplayed structural references. In this sense, the Prairie style foreshadowed Modernism more literally than Craftsman, and after a century some of its best examples still appear "modern" today.

Like Craftsman, the Prairie style was primarily applied to residential designs, but it did have an influence on larger public and commercial buildings. Until the Modern movement took hold in America (mostly after 1930), the Prairie style reigned as the most progressive ever seen or produced here, and was also recognized abroad as a true American "original." With the arrival from Europe of the spare and sleek International style (mostly applied to commercial buildings), our Modern period was firmly launched, and any progressive edge then that lingered around the Prairie style was diminished. However, it is notable that advanced architectural circles in Europe before 1930, largely centered in Germany, had already been influenced by this progressive American style. Forced to flee the repression of Nazism, some the most important world leaders of modern architecture immigrated to America, before World War II. This assured the ongoing dissemination of Modernism that dominated the remainder of the twentieth century, and continues today.

Within the boundaries of somewhat loosely defined aesthetic tenets, Prairie-style homes became as

Figure 60.

GEORGE BARTON HOUSE, BUFFALO, NEW YORK (1903).

This characteristic Prairie-style home in the Parkside area was designed by Frank Lloyd Wright for George Barton and his wife, Delta Martin Barton. Common to many of Wright's designs of this period are the narrow-profile "Roman" brick and shallow hipped-roof forms, which reinforce the style's typical horizontal emphasis. Exaggerated in height, the brick walls visually compress the second floor and windows into a frieze-like banding. Not apparent in this view, the home's cruciform (cross-shaped) plan includes two single-story wings; one at left precisely bisects the two-story part, and another low wing (out of view) containing the kitchen and service areas, is on its opposite side. The front door opens to an entry hall, which adjoins the open porch at left. A sequence of flowing public spaces combines the living, dining, and library areas. Four bedrooms and a bath comprise the second floor. Mrs. Barton was the sister of Mrs. Darwin Martin, and this home was oriented towards the neighboring Darwin Martin House (to the left), one of Wright's largest Prairie houses. A unique architectural ensemble, it included a long pergola-covered walkway linking the larger house to a conservatory and garage, across a large expanse of garden areas. These elements were subsequently destroyed, and replaced by an intrusive 1950s apartment building. Now undergoing a major restoration that will recreate them, this important Wright compound is open to the public (see Resources, page 189).

Figure 61 (above).

WEBB HOUSE, OAK PARK, ILLINOIS (1910).

*Designed by Chicago architect Henry K. Holsman, this substantial home was built for George D. Webb. Although more complex in its detailing than the house seen in Figure 60, it has similar Prairie-style features, including a hipped roof (here used with dormers), and first-floor brick walls rising to the sills of the second-floor windows. Published in a 1913 book called **Modern American Homes** by Hermann Valentin von Holst, this photograph accompanied an article entitled "An Attractive Country Residence Combining Elegance With Good Taste," which stated that the house ". . . is an excellent illustration of the beauty of preserving simple lines even in costly houses." The corner home's driveway is entered from the street on the far left side, and runs behind the house. Lined with square brick columns, a covered breezeway connects the house and garage (not visible in Figure 62). The nearby grouping of corner windows are in a breakfast room that adjoins the dining room (see Figure 64).*

Figure 62 (opposite).

RECENT VIEW OF THE WEBB HOUSE.

This shows off the textural effect created by the varying shades in the brick that occur on its first-floor walls. In a departure from the Prairie style that implies a Colonial Revival influence, a pair of classically inspired columns supports the gable of the small front entry portico. A large covered screened porch at far left (which adjoins the living room) also connects to the front door by way of a raised, open terrace on either side of the front door (more visible in Figure 61). An aspiration of many Prairie-style designs was to foster such seamless links between interior and exterior living spaces. The dining room in Figure 64 is on the right side of the front door. Lit by dormer windows, the spacious attic level contains the servants' quarters, but is primarily occupied by a large, informal family living space that includes a fireplace. Such areas could also serve as a game room or children's playroom.

recognizable as Craftsman examples. However, Prairie was never as popular a style with the average homeowner, and remained on the outer fringe of mainstream taste. Although exceptions occurred, the Prairie style was less subject to as many outside influences (i.e., historic crossovers styles) that were commonly blended with Craftsman style. This sustained a progressive aura around the Prairie style for a longer period.

From the Chicago School

The city of Chicago was already well established as a center of progressive architecture before the Prairie style emerged in its environs just a few years prior to 1900. Seeking to rebuild following the famously disastrous fire of 1871 that destroyed most of its commercial core, the city became a magnet for architects, designers, and the construction trades. Some of America's finest architects and engineers relocated to Chicago, and their influence on other architects in that area proved to be enormous. The collective work of these progressive architectural pioneers has since been described as the "Chicago school," referring not to an actual school, but to their home city and its important collection of influential new architecture at the end of the nineteenth century.

At first, Chicago's post-fire building boom was concentrated on the construction of commercial buildings (i.e., office buildings and warehouses), which were needed in great numbers to revitalize business. Advances in structural engineering forwarded by William Lebaron Jenney led to the emergence of steel framing, which would replace the use of ponderous, all-masonry construction for multi-story buildings. A leading architectural firm of Chicago's boom years, Adler & Sullivan is credited with pioneering key projects that firmly established the American skyscraper. Pairing the engineering and technical skills of Dankmar Adler (1844–1900) with the designs of a brilliant young architect named Louis Henri Sullivan (1856–1924), the firm produced ground-breaking, high-rise steel-frame building designs by the early 1890s. Other Chicago firms soon followed their lead, and the American urban landscape has never been the same. Besides his prodigious creative abilities, Sullivan was a charismatic teacher to the young architects who came under his firm's employ—most famously Frank Lloyd Wright.

The Prairie Style and Frank Lloyd Wright

No discussion of the Prairie style or its origins can be complete without mention of Frank Lloyd Wright (1867–1959), now arguably considered the most famous American-born architect in our history. There is no question that he was the Prairie style's most important and influential proponent. A succession of innovative residential projects that Wright designed in and around the Chicago area, mostly completed before 1910, comprise "textbook" examples of that style. While he is certainly the architect who is most often associated with Prairie design, some of Wright's contemporaries also made important contributions.

While still employed by Adler & Sullivan, Wright had already designed some houses on his own, but his illustrious solo career began in earnest after he left the firm. Throughout his long life, Wright readily acknowledged Louis Sullivan as his mentor, and as the most important influence on his career.

(continued on page 81)

Figure 63 (opposite).

STAIRCASE IN THE WEBB HOUSE.

Opposite the front door, the main staircase is framed by an arched opening as wide as the entry hall. On angled walls to either side of the stairs are doors set within the high wainscot paneling. The left-hand door connects to a powder room, a secondary entrance (accessible from the rear driveway), and the basement stairs. The door on the right opens to the library. The two-light ceiling fixture is one of several original to the house. Tall and narrow art-glass windows with Prairie-style geometric motifs backlight a built-in window seat on the landing. With its harmonious coloring and whimsically contrasting pattern, a recreated wallpaper by English Arts and Crafts architect/designer C. F. A. Voysey makes an unusual but effective counterpoint to the simple linearity of the art glass. The entry hall's "pendant" frieze, another period wallpaper reproduction, is partly visible above the arch. On the stairs, a bordered carpet runner adapts a vintage William Morris pattern.

Figure 64.

DINING ROOM IN THE WEBB HOUSE.

This room connects to the entry hall through pocket doors set into a wide opening. The doors have simple leaded art-glass designs of crossing lines set into their upper lights. To ensure privacy, unleaded panes of swirly slag glass that match the art-glass background are used in the doors' lower lights. The upper art-glass design repeats in an otherwise solid wood swinging door to the kitchen (at far left) and on a library door (out of view, at near left). Mostly in clear glass, the design is repeated on the french doors at right, which lead to a rear corner breakfast room (see Figure 61). All the doors' upper lights are aligned with the top of the wainscot paneling. The box-beam ceiling is wallpapered and bordered; the frieze, with a lion and dove motif and a quote from the Book of Isaiah, reproduces a 1900 pattern by noted English artist and designer Walter Crane. The fireplace surround has original matte-glazed tiles that blend muted ochres and browns. Above the tile, a recessed display niche supplants a mantel shelf. Published with the exterior (Figure 61), a 1910 dining room photograph shows this same ceiling fixture, as well as a now-missing built-in sideboard along the left wall. Such period photos are of invaluable use for future restoration purposes, but it is rare for them to be available to the current owners of the same house.

Figure 65.

K.T. SNYDER HOUSE, MINNEAPOLIS, MINNESOTA (1915).

Local architect Kirby T. Snyder designed and built this home for his own residence. Modest in scale, it manages to command its corner lot. Its visibility is expanded by a long brick retaining wall, which creates a pedestal for the house and extends to a rear service alley. Partway down the block, an attached peaked-roof garage is recessed into the wall. In its proportions and roof details, the one-car garage resembles those of the enclosed entry porch on the right. While outwardly this home appears to be a fairly conventional interpretation of Prairie forms, its interior showcases the uniquely personal style statements that Snyder chose to make in his own private environment.

Figure 66 (opposite).

ENTRY PORCH IN THE SNYDER HOUSE.

Once inside the copper-sheathed front door (partly seen at far right), the architect's unusual sense of detailing begins to emerge in this room. A practical consideration because of the area's harsh winters, the porch is enclosed on the front and left sides by bands of ingeniously folding casement windows of Prairie-style art glass. To maximize light and visibility, mostly clear glass is used in their leaded designs. In the exposed peak of the roof gable, a rather moody vintage landscape mural is hand-painted on a grid of leaded-glass panels. The floor's durable terra-cotta tile, inset with a darker border, makes a sensible finish choice in this transitional indoor-outdoor space. The current owners have furnished the porch as a sitting area, with a dining table at left, thus expanding options for its use. The painted cloud-motif ceiling is a later addition.

Figure 67

STAIR HALL IN THE SNYDER HOUSE.

In its almost playful quirkiness, this area evokes a Postmodernist impression or, perhaps, with its unexpected richness, the lobby décor of a vintage public building. In any case, most previous expectations of Prairie-style interiors tend to dissolve into wide-eyed wonderment at the juxtaposition of styles and influences seen here. Marble appears where wood is typically employed in other domestic interiors of this period. White-and-gray Carrara marble is used for the floor, baseboard, stair stringers, newel posts, and moldings of wall panels that recall high board-and-batten wainscoting. The panels are inset with a contrasting peach-colored marble. A Colonial Revival influence is implied by the turned wooden spindles. A towering stairwell window has leaded art-glass designs in linear asymmetrical arrangements with brightly hued accents. Classically inspired dentil moldings of plaster surround the partly curving ceiling outline; the light fixture is original. At upper right, a hand-painted landscape scene framed by ornate plaster moldings is one of several similar panels occurring in the upstairs hall area. Detailed to match existing examples elsewhere in the house, the vented built-in wooden cabinet was added by the current owner. Worn original velvet cladding on the handrails was replaced with new leather.

Figure 68 (opposite).

DETAIL OF DINING (TOWARD LIVING ROOM) IN THE SNYDER HOUSE.

The stair hall's stylish but improbable tone continues in the original schemes of the main public rooms. In the foreground, the walnut-paneled dining room has ceiling beams with metallic accents applied to their complex classical moldings. One of a pair, the tall built-in china cabinet with geometric leaded-glass doors flanks a broad opening to the living room. Set back to back are matching cabinets facing the living room side. Special hinges allow for pairs of french doors to be fully folded back. The low-slung living room fireplace, in stone and brick with a mottled green glazed tile hearth, has a screen of pivoting cast-iron doors with open, stylized cornstalk motifs that was added by the current owners. The wall above has a central recessed panel for artwork, and a pair of display niches. Oversized, lantern-like art-glass sconces are carefully integrated into the room's perimeter wood molding above. Abstracted classical forms stylized with an Art Nouveau twist enliven a low-relief plaster frieze encircling the room. To the right of the fireplace, french doors open to the stair hall. Next to them is a tall built-in cabinet, one of another dual-sided pair that matches those seen in the dining room. Supporting an open shelf that spans the space, the living room's pair of cabinets frames a central opening to a music room at the front of the house.

(continued from page 75)

In 1897, joining other professional peers who were similarly influenced by Sullivan, Wright became a charter member of the Chicago Arts and Crafts Society. His public support of this group suggests that he was both familiar with and sympathetic to the tenets of the movement. Otherwise steering clear of group thinking, he was careful throughout his life to position himself as an "original" whenever possible. In what some perceived as an affront to the movement, Wright presented a manifesto in 1901 called "The Art and Craft of the Machine." While he agreed that the use of natural materials was admirable, Wright argued that machines, if employed in the correct context, could actually help achieve much of the same goals concerning the production of modern-day craft goods that had been sought by English movement leader William Morris, who had died in 1896. Prophetically, what Wright opined in 1901 closely paralleled a future tenet of the Modern movement in its early idealistic years, which stressed the importance of creating models of superior design for any goods to be mass-produced by machine.

Wright's first independent commission, the Winslow House (1893) in River Forest, Illinois, was a groundbreaking design that foreshadowed elements of the Prairie style. As his design work evolved, so did his interest in and expression of other influences. These went beyond the abstract concepts of "organic architecture" he had gleaned from Sullivan. The arts and architecture of Japan resonated strongly with Wright, and this influence is especially apparent in the interiors of his Prairie homes. Recalling the open planning of traditional Japanese dwellings, these free-flowing spaces seemed to reinvent the concept in America of what constituted a room.

Other than acknowledging his debt to Sullivan, Wright was routinely cryptic about sources of his inspiration. Therefore, it makes interesting speculation to guess at how much Wright may have been influenced or inspired by what he saw at the 1893 World's Columbian Exposition in Chicago. Possibly a factor in influencing his future work was a reduced-scale replica of a timber-framed Japanese shrine constructed by master craftsmen from Japan, along with Japanese furniture and other decorative arts that were on display. The same shrine structure had certainly impressed and later influenced architects Charles and Henry Greene, who had also visited the Chicago event. It is likely that Wright's affinity for Japanese design eventually helped him secure his commission for the famed Imperial Hotel (1916–1922) in Tokyo (now demolished). Along the way, he also expanded his business opportunities to become one of America's primary dealers in Japanese woodblock prints.

The Prairie School

Separate from the "Chicago School" described earlier, the group of architects and their work that reflects the Prairie style are sometimes referred to as the "Prairie School." Notably, it was Frank Lloyd Wright who actually coined this term, in a 1938 reference to his own work completed during the early period (1893–1910) of his independent practice. The term is now more generally applied to include other architects' work, and its duration is therefore more broadly interpreted.

Some examples of the Prairie style, especially those that developed further afield from its Chicago sources and Sullivan's or Wright's inspiration, were subject to other influences. While such examples are interesting to analyze (mostly as Prairie crossovers or hybrids), most lack the compelling clarity of the style's early, most definitive examples. By the 1920s, some versions of Prairie-style designs were persisting for inexpensive plan book houses, including bungalows. Although these homes' simple lines differentiated them from that decade's more popular historical revival styles, by then (much like Craftsman), Prairie was no longer considered one of the latest housing trends.

Other Prairie School Players

Several other architects of Wright's generation were also inspired by Sullivan's influence, and some achieved a respectable degree of prominence on their own. Among these other progressive architects who forged independent careers in the Chicago area was George Washington Maher (1864–1926), whose philosophic approach to creating architecture paralleled Sullivan's. Concurrent with Wright, Maher also became an important early figure in the development of the Prairie style. Even before 1890, Maher had written about the need for a "new American architecture," free of the constraining influences of historic revivalism. By 1897, he had designed a significant early example of a Prairie-style house for the John Farsen family in Oak Park, Illinois. Called "Pleasant Home," it is now open to the public as a house museum (see Resources, page 190). Long overshadowed in that area by the proximity of Wright and his work, Maher today deserves more credit and recognition for his contributions to American architecture and design.

Other significant contributors to the development of the Prairie style were George Grant Elmslie (1869–1952) and William Gray Purcell (1880–1965). Elmslie was Louis Sullivan's right-hand man for many years, and was responsible for interpreting and designing much of the distinctive "organic" ornament that became Sullivan's signature on his later projects. For a shorter time, Purcell had also worked

(continued on page 89)

Figure 69.

HOUSE IN MINNEAPOLIS, MINNESOTA (1915).

With hipped-roof forms of terra-cotta tile, this home shows simple Prairie-style massing. Dorr and Dorr, a local architectural firm, designed the house for a sloping site that overlooks a picturesque lake. A rear extension that includes an attached garage (accessible from a rear service alley) is glimpsed at far left. The battered (sloping) buttress detailing seen on the home's corners at left implies a British Arts and Crafts influence, such as that of architect/designer C. F. A. Voysey. This area's climate determined that the front porch was glass-enclosed. Projecting second-floor windows at the center are in a bedroom that was likely an original sleeping porch. The current owners have recently landscaped the site with large boulders and specimen plantings composed around an expansive lawn. It now includes the neighboring lot to the left, which was recently acquired to accommodate a major future expansion. Brimming with colorful flowers, large Prairie-style concrete urns create a welcoming effect at the raised terrace by the front door. Out of view to the right, a series of matching urns also flanks the front walk and stairs.

Figure 70 (opposite).

REAR OF THE MINNEAPOLIS HOUSE.

Seen from a gate to the rear service alley, the home's asymmetry this side gives it a more informal quality. At left, a battered (slop brick buttress marks a corner of the rear wing that delineates the building's predominantly L-shaped plan. Creating a more intim sense of scale, the home's mass is reduced by the single-story oct nal extension (an original feature) at right. This space was built sunroom but is now used as a family/media room (see Figure 7 Topped by arching transoms, oversized pairs of casement windo occur on five of that room's eight sides. The angled steps of the brick terrace echo its octagonal form. Flanked by fixed doors use sidelights, a french door opens to a passage that connects to the fa media room at right, the entry hall ahead, and the kitchen to th The large, open part of the garden (seen in Figure 69) is to the Detailed in a squared-off Prairie fashion, the home's copper gu have acquired their handsome blue-green patina over time.

Figure 71.

ENTRY HALL IN THE MINNEAPOLIS HOUSE.

The entry hall, a pivotal hub of circulation that adjoins the enclosed front porch through an inner front door (out of view) to the far left, is mostly open to the living room. The wide opening's horizontality is continued in a three-part window overlooking the large side yard. In the living room's far corner, an arched doorway that leads to the family/media room is one of two flanking a fireplace. Useful as display shelves, low walls on either side of the wide opening are terminated by taller square posts that serve as pedestals. The one on the right also doubles as the staircase's newel post, and its flat-capped detailing repeats on the stair's smaller posts. The lower landing forms a raised, room-wide platform that also connects to the passage leading to the rear garden (see Figure 70). Behind a square-spindled railing at right, one of the rear entry's door-sized sidelights is visible. This railing also forms the back of a substantial built-in bench facing the entry hall. The dining room is to the right. Recently crafted, the entry hall's art-glass lantern adapts typical Prairie-style forms.

Figure 72.

LIVING ROOM IN THE MINNEAPOLIS HOUSE.

The wide window at right, a variation of the so-called "Chicago window," is comprised of a fixed central panel and side windows that open. Similar three-part modular group-ings were employed in that city's early skyscrapers. A distinctive pair of Prairie-style chairs is part of this room's mix of furnishings, which also includes some Craftsman and Asian pieces. A Prairie-style wall sconce, one of two flanking the window, is next to a tall vintage Japanese tansu (cabinet) in the corner. The proportions of the perimeter ceiling mold-ing are continued in the small-scale box beams that span the room's width and help offset its length. Bordered by narrow divided lights, french doors in folding pairs are used in a wide doorway connecting the enclosed front porch to the living room. Lined with casement windows and overlooking the lake, the porch includes a sitting area filled with wicker furniture. Adding considerable extra living space, the porch improves the home's circulation flow for entertaining. The entry hall and inner front door are out of view to the left.

Figure 73.

FAMILY/MEDIA ROOM IN THE MINNEAPOLIS HOUSE.

This airy space, originally a sunroom, is used by the current owners as a family/media room. Its walls extend unbroken onto a coved ceiling, creating the effect of a shallow dome. As part of the recent remodel, walls and ceiling received a "Tiffany" finish, a decorative painting technique popular in the early twentieth century. It employs multiple colors subtly layered and blended, to create a mottled effect similar to an art pottery glaze. Ambient lighting is provided by vintage wall sconces with an Art Deco influence. When outfitted as a media room, built-in cushioned seating was added on three of the angled sides, preserving open space in the center for lounging on the carpeted floor. Small retractable sliding tables, a convenient detail built into the seating units, also obviate the need for any extra furniture. With typical geometric motifs adapted into its bold Prairie form, a tall custom built-in cabinet (partly seen at left) stylishly conceals the television and music system components.

Figure 74.

KITCHEN IN THE MINNEAPOLIS HOUSE.

An homage to the Prairie style, this kitchen design was a major portion of the recent remodel. Small, original service and utility areas were combined to allow space for a large open dining area. Improving indoor-outdoor flow, french doors were added along its left side (out of view), which open onto the terrace and rear garden area (see Figure 70). Down one step, the dining area has a floor of durable ceramic tile, whose mottled texture and cinnamon-color glaze inspired the lighter sponge-painted walls. Recessed in the far corner is a built-in sideboard near an open doorway that leads to the laundry and attached garage. At the left end of the peninsula dividing the two areas, the square post and side panel were detailed to adapt elements of the front stairway (see Figure 71). Soft green soapstone counters harmonize with handmade field, accent, and border tiles used in the panel behind the range (beneath a handcrafted copper hood), and elsewhere on the backsplash, which is inset with a small window that opens. Unifying the space, crossbeams align with the woodwork on the side walls. Backlit at frieze height on both sides of the room, are leaded geometric art-glass panels set between the beams. A linear design of smaller-scaled moldings overlays each ceiling panel. To integrate Prairie-style pendant lighting into this design, moldings wrap down and around the beams at each fixture, reinforcing the rhythmic repetition of the room's key design elements.

(continued from page 82)

in Sullivan's firm, and embraced many of his employer's concepts shared by Elmslie. After relocating to Minneapolis, Purcell formed a partnership with another architect, George Feick Jr. (1881–1945), and in 1910 invited Elmslie, by then independent, to join them as a third partner. The firm of Purcell, Feick, and Elmslie continued until 1913, when Feick left, and continued as Purcell and Elmslie until 1921. The firm's most notable Minneapolis commissions include the E. L. Powers House (1910), and the Purcell-Cutts House (1913), which was created the same year Feick left. Both are important and innovative landmarks of the Prairie style. Today, the Purcell-Cutts House is open to the public as a house museum (see Resources, page 190).

Prairie-Style Forms and Features

Horizontality is the most characteristic quality of Prairie style. This is usually created by the roof, which is typically hipped (pyramidal), and reads as a plain, spreading, solid form. Dormers are sometimes seen, but are less typical (SEE FIGURE 61–62).

Because most Prairie roofs have a fairly shallow pitch, those of some homes (at close range) may appear as if completely flat. While some were also built with gabled roofs, these are much less common, and their style identity is established by other characteristic features.

Prairie-style homes were both small and large. For exterior finish, the best of the period examples often utilized narrow-profile "Roman" brick. The overall proportions of some homes were manipulated by extending the first-floor brick walls up to the second-floor windowsills in an unbroken line, thereby exaggerating the height of the first floor (SEE FIGURES 60–62). This reinforces the design's horizontality and groundedness. In such cases, the second floor outwardly appears as a narrow band-like area (like a frieze), usually only the height of its windows. Above a first floor of brick, the wall areas adjacent to second-floor windows were often finished in painted stucco. Prairie-style homes in areas with warmer climates were more likely to be entirely faced with stucco.

In overall massing, many of the more modest examples tend to be low-slung, single-story compositions with simple rectangular plans, which describes typical Prairie-style bungalows. On such smaller homes, the hipped roof usually appears as a more dominant part of the overall form. This most basic shape strongly influenced many generic "Ranch house" designs of the post–World War II period. Contained within a simple box-like volume, some two-story Prairie designs were closely related to the upright form of a typical American foursquare (SEE FIGURE 7).

Larger building sites allowed for more expansive Prairie-style homes, with the outwardly spreading configurations associated with the finest examples of the style. Many of these designs are arranged to include both one and two-story sections, sometimes in L- or T-shaped plans (SEE FIGURE 60). If space allows, it is a characteristic Prairie feature to extend the lines of a house into the landscape by low walls,

Figure 75.

JAMES AND CORINNE WILLIAMS HOUSE, SPOKANE, WASHINGTON (1911).

Local architect Albert Held was commissioned by Mr. and Mrs. Williams to design their home as a gracious place to entertain. In overall massing, this historic South Hill area house has a strong Prairie influence in the hipped form of its roof and in the dominant horizontal emphasis of its composition. While the well-balanced façade appears symmetrical, a porte-cochère (partly visible) extends over the driveway on the left side. The Prairie style is also evoked by the sturdy, square brick columns supporting the front porch roof. These are integral with the low, concrete-capped railing walls that rise uninterrupted from the foundation line. In a crossover blending, Craftsman-style detailing occurs in the use of exposed rafter tails and in the form and detailing of a covered balcony at the center of the second floor, which creates a focal point for the façade. A solid, shingled railing wall supports groupings of three square wooden columns at each front corner, which appear to be linked by "through-tenon" detailing near their tops. Without this balcony, the house would resemble a stretched-out version of a foursquare. Its centrally-placed, hipped-roof attic dormer is a common feature of many examples of that ubiquitous early-twentieth-century American housing type.

Figure 76 (opposite).

STAIRCASE IN THE WILLIAMS HOUSE.

Executed in quartersawn oak, this striking staircase incorporates a built-in bench, a common Craftsman-style feature, at its base. More unexpected is the oddly stylish design of the newel posts, whose effect is amplified through repetition and proximity. Pendant-like geometric forms in their incised decoration are Prairie-influenced details, but the small repeating squares recall designs by progressive "Glasgow School" and Vienna Secessionist designers. Below their caps, each post terminates in curious rounded forms at its corners, which recall the form of wooden spoons. Plain square spindles occur here in two sizes. Used vertically for the railing's primary structural support, the thicker spindles are also used for secondary cross-pieces placed horizontally a few inches below the handrails. This detail adds design interest by grouping the smaller spindles within framed panels that step up in tandem with the stairs.

Figure 77.

VILLA ORIZABA, SAN DIEGO, CALIFORNIA (1886; AS REMODELED, C1915).

Beneath a spreading hipped roof, the symmetrical façade of this Prairie-style house makes a strong horizontal statement. Two single-story projections on either side create open balconies above groupings of oversized first-floor windows in the public rooms facing the street. With a monumental effect, the long flight of front stairs aligns with the width of the massively scaled front porch. It is detailed with squared forms, shallow panel insets, and solid railing walls around its second-floor balcony. A line of raised flat molding carried across the façade on either side defines the first floor. This existing structure is actually an extreme remodel of a smaller Victorian-era house. Its original roof framing is still visible within the newer attic that was constructed around and over it. The house was first built by the captain of a long-running steamship called the Orizaba (the home's namesake). When his ship was being remodeled, he was able to salvage a complete Eastlake-style staircase from it, which he adapted as the main staircase of this house. During the later remodel, the original interior was largely reconfigured and obscured by Craftsman-era detailing. But the Orizaba's staircase still remains in the entry hall and is a fascinating functional artifact of this city's maritime history.

whose building materials echo those of the house. Often topped by strategically placed concrete urns of appropriate Prairie design, such walls are used to enclose outdoor terraces, or to define front entry walks and stairs.

Quite opposite from the Craftsman style, the purest examples of Prairie style generally feature concealed structural elements to achieve their signature clean-lined look. Roof eaves are boxed in with unexposed rafter tails. The eaves are cantilevered outward without additional visible support such as brackets. When columns appear, they are square (not tapering), and tend to be fairly massive in their proportion. Windows are most often the casement (swinging) type, and are typically grouped in multiples. Double-hung (vertically sliding) windows may sometimes be included as well.

Inside, the best examples have flowing, interconnected public spaces. As with the Craftsman style, a fireplace usually occupies a central place of honor in the living room. Fireplaces are most likely to be faced in plain brick, usually matching the home's exterior finish. The use of some built-in furniture is another commonality with Craftsman-style interiors. Most typical are built-in benches, window seats, bookcases, and dining room sideboards. Woodwork detailing tends to be quite

Figure 78.

LIVING ROOM IN VILLA ORIZABA.

This room shows no trace of the home's previous incarnation. The wall sconces date to the time of its major remodel in the mid-1910s. To the left of the grouping of three wide windows that face the street, the spacious entry hall (out of view) features box beams and a welcoming Craftsman-style fireplace, in contrast with the steamship Orizaba's ornate staircase. This same grouping of windows is also seen in Figure 77 (on the left side of the front porch). Across the entry hall, the dining room also has three matching windows that balance the façade. Recently, all the windows of this unusually large room were fitted with new linen curtains. Appliquéd and embroidered by hand, small Arts and Crafts motifs appear as subtle accents on each pair. Not visible in this view is a generously scaled inglenook for the fireplace (recessed into the wall opposite the front windows). Craftsman-style reproductions comprise most of the furniture and accessories throughout this room.

simple in form and squared-off in profile. Although Prairie interiors generally made a less intensive use of woodwork than Craftsman ones, natural wood finishes were also favored. Box-beamed ceilings were sometimes employed, but plain ceilings with substantial perimeter wood moldings were more typical. In the most definitive period examples, leaded art glass as interior accents is prevalent, with linear, highly stylized geometric motifs being the most characteristic. Some Prairie homes have art-glass lighting fixtures that repeat design motifs of the windows.

As a word of caution, many vintage Prairie houses don't lend themselves particularly well to new additions. In some cases, it is extremely difficult to successfully match the existing materials of the homes' original finishes. Unlike the case with Craftsman, the Prairie style is less routinely used today as a model for newly constructed homes. Notably, when this does happen, it is more likely to occur in and around the vicinity of its upper-midwest birthplace. However, anyone living in a good period example will likely concur that adapting to modern life in a Prairie-style home is nearly effortless, because they express a truly timeless design sensibility.

Figure 79.

GRAYCLIFF (ISABELLE MARTIN HOUSE), DERBY, NEW YORK (1927).

Frank Lloyd Wright designed this home as a summer residence for Mr. and Mrs. Darwin Martin. Wright had designed the Martin's large 1904 Prairie home in Buffalo, which adjoins his 1903 George Barton House (see Figure 60). Along with that important compound, Graycliff is now open to the public as a house museum. Darwin Martin insisted that his wife should be considered the client, thereby linking her name to this house. Isabelle Martin had poor eyesight, and she found their Buffalo home too dark. Therefore, Graycliff was to have abundant daylight. While completed long after Wright's Prairie period was officially over, Graycliff manages to embody many similar planning considerations that guided his true Prairie-home designs. For example, it shares the Prairie style's horizontal emphasis, hipped-roof forms, open main-floor plan, and flowing indoor-outdoor spaces. Perched beside a steep stone cliff overlooking Lake Erie, Graycliff was named for its dramatic site. Viewed on approach (the lake is behind it), the home's welcoming informality befits a vacation home. Mostly stuccoed, the building utilizes irregular local stone for some wall areas, and the columns of a projecting porte-cochère that shelters the front entry. A stone fountain between the columns directs water into a naturalistic pond. At far right, a stucco garden wall links the house to a garage structure with living quarters above (out of view), which completes Graycliff's L-shaped composition on approach to this front side.

Figure 80.

SECOND FLOOR GALLERY IN GRAYCLIFF.

This long, peaked-roof gallery runs parallel to the façade and adjoins the family bedrooms along the left, which overlook the lake. Natural light floods the space through southerly windows on the right (see Figure 80), which have outlooks over the front lawn and garden areas. At the far end, a door opens to a separate service area, including two servant's bedrooms and bathroom, that connects to the kitchen area below via a servants' stairs. At the opposite end is the main staircase, descending to the entry hall that adjoins the **porte cochère** in front. As befits a summer house, the Martins furnished it casually, without any Wright-designed furniture as had characterized their Buffalo home. While much of Graycliff's interior awaits complete restoration, it has retained many of its original features, and further improvements are now well underway.

Figure 81.

FRONT DETAIL OF GRAYCLIFF.

A closer view shows the area to the right of the **porte cochère** seen in Figure 79. Buffered by a low stone wall enclosure that incorporates a parallel planter, a long covered terrace is recessed into the façade. Visible above are a series of windows lining the second-floor gallery (see Figure 80). To maximize its natural light, Graycliff has a linear floor plan and is only one room deep. Light seen through french doors at left is passing through the living room from behind the house. An enormous stone fireplace divides the large living room from the dining room on the far right. The doors in the stone wall at the end of the terrace open to the kitchen, which adjoins other utility areas and servant's stairs at the rear. After Graycliff was acquired in 1951 by the Piarists, a Catholic brotherhood and teaching order, the entire terrace area was obscured by its enclosure as a chapel. In 1999, the property was purchased by the Graycliff Conservancy, which is now guiding the home's restoration and future uses. The reopened terrace area has largely restored the home's original front appearance as Wright intended it.

Figure 82.

END DETAIL OF GRAYCLIFF.

The blue water of Lake Erie stretches along the horizon in this view, which shows the home's west-side elevation. The cantilevered balcony with solid railing walls is also visible on the left side of the front façade (see Figure 79). Wright incorporated similarly detailed balconies in both earlier and later projects. The balcony is part of Darwin Martin's private suite, which includes a bedroom on the lakeside corner, a bathroom, and a sleeping porch on the far right. Under the balcony is a window-lined sunroom that connects to the living room. In the stone wall at right, a window lights a guest bathroom. The shed-roof detail above it, combined with the visual weight of the stonework, helps anchor the design. In a Prairie gesture, the home is extended into the landscape by low stone walls, which enclose a sunken garden. Out of view on the rear side, french doors open to a raised terrace, fusing the primary public rooms with the outdoors. Creating a strong axial connection between the rear elevation of the house and lake, similar low stone walls were used by Wright to outline a long recessed lawn area (which he originally called an "esplanade"), and to frame the water view.

AMERICAN HISTORICISM

Our Own Colonial & Spanish Revival Styles

Overview of America's Historic Styles

Considering the range of popular early twentieth century styles, it is apparent that the home-building industry didn't want to leave prospective buyers without choices. By the 1920s, these had been greatly expanded, but in the earliest years of the 1900s, they were more limited. At that time, the appeal of modernity, with its progressive design and a new way of living, attracted some to the Craftsman or Prairie styles. Later, shifting public taste, a more conservative outlook, or perhaps nostalgia for a vanished past, increasingly drew others to historic revival styles. This chapter's focus is on the historic styles that reflect aspects of America's own history.

America's fascination with housing styles inspired by the past was certainly not a new phenomenon. A succession of historic revival styles had occurred throughout the preceding Victorian era. Public taste would be fixated on one for a time, only to yearn for another one more fashionable some years later. Unlike the veritable style smorgasbord of the post-1900 period, the Victorian styles had an average popular duration of ten to twenty years apiece. Overlapping occurred between these styles; one might still be in fashion in the West when the next style craze had already gripped the East. In order of their appearance, the nineteenth-century lineup of popular housing styles based in historicism included the Greek and Gothic Revivals, and the Italianate, Second Empire, and Romanesque Revival styles. The eclecticism of the Queen Anne style versus the Colonial Revival's chaste demeanor vied for national dominance toward that century's end.

But these weren't all of the Victorian era's styles. Among the others, only the Stick (or Stick-Eastlake) style was conceived outside the historic-revival loop, making it the most progressive and "proto-modern" of its era. Its use of visible structural elements such as brackets in its designs foreshadowed the Craftsman style by more than two decades. The Shingle style straddled both sides of 1900. Although it was inspired by utilitarian shingled structures of the Colonial era, it was largely free of historic revival influences when interpreted for its own sake. Before 1900, the Shingle style was often combined with elements of the Queen Anne and Colonial Revival. After that, it was more often blended with the Craftsman style. The Mission Revival also occurred both before and after 1900, and was the first style to be specifically linked to the history of the American West. In this sense, it anticipated the later Spanish Colonial Revival style.

(continued on page 101)

Figure 83.

HOUSE IN MILWAUKEE, WISCONSIN (C1914).

The symmetrical brick façade and simplified classical detailing of this Washington Heights area home evokes the Colonial Revival style. The arching forms of the attic dormer and front porch roof, which create a barrel-vault ceiling over the front door, are also consistent with that style. Despite the side-facing gables of its main roof, the home's rectangular massing and single central dormer suggest the basic form of a foursquare, which more typically has a hipped (pyramidal) roof. Detailed with recessed panels, the square, tapering porch columns show a Craftsman influence that also occurs inside (see Figures 84–86). Faced with matching crown moldings, shallow overhangs above pairs of windows extend the porch's roofline to either side, and add horizontal definition to the first floor.

Figure 84.

LIVING ROOM IN THE MILWAUKEE HOUSE.

Elements of the home's façade reappear in this room, and include the arching forms employed on the far wall and the earth-colored brick used for the fireplace. Although understated, a Colonial Revival influence is seen in the room's molding profiles, especially in its crown molding. Craftsman elements are suggested in the wooden mantel's simply detailed corbels, and in the pair of built-in cabinets with leaded-glass doors. Unlike the built-ins that flank the fireplaces of most Craftsman-style interiors, this alternate placement allows for larger windows and more daylight by the fireplace. Between the cabinets, a wide arched doorway opens into an inviting sunroom that overlooks the rear garden. Similar to those of the cabinets, plain leaded grids are used in a pair of arch-topped french doors. From the central entry hall, this room is entered through a wide opening out of view on the left, across the entry hall from the dining room (seen in Figure 85).

Figure 85.

DINING ROOM IN THE MILWAUKEE HOUSE.

With more of a Craftsman feeling, this room also has a cozier sense of scale than the living room. For continuity, the quartersawn oak woodwork repeats the profiles of the living room's crown molding as well as its door and window casings. Set between a pair of doors, a built-in sideboard with an arching top recalls the form of the front porch, and was detailed to integrate with the high wainscoting and plate rail surrounding the room. On the far left, a door (out of view) leads to the kitchen through a butler's pantry, while the door at right is for a closet. Both the sideboard's upper cabinet doors, and the french doors at right, have leaded-glass grids similar to those used in the living room. However, this wide doorway has a squared-off top and space-saving pocket (sliding) doors. Across the entry hall, the living room is glimpsed through another wide doorway. Partly visible is one of two partial-height paneled walls that frame this opening, which are being used as display shelves. Recently custom-made for this room is a set of strikingly angular Prairie-style dining furniture. The ceiling fixture is of the period.

Figure 86.

KITCHEN IN THE MILWAUKEE HOUSE.

Interpreting the simplicity of the Craftsman style with a contemporary twist, this design transformed a poorly arranged and inappropriate kitchen. Pale maple floors, natural birch cabinetry, and a light, cheerful paint scheme ensure brightness. Recalling bungalow planning, a handy breakfast nook was created within the compact space by adding a side bay window. This feature replicates the overall proportions of the original windows as well as the simple leaded grids in their upper sashes. More accessible here than lift-up seats, the nook's benches incorporate deep storage drawers that extend from their ends. Both the built-in dining table and freestanding work island borrow their square-spindled screens and through-tenon detailing from Craftsman-style furniture. Pairs of small corbel-like elements accent the tops of cabinets and other woodwork. A deep farmhouse-type sink, made of stainless steel to match the room's appliances, is set into a darkly colored concrete counter. In the far corner, a door to the butler's pantry also connects to the dining room.

(continued from page 96)

It should be noted here that the Rustic style, which also occurred on either side of 1900, may be considered as another American influence on architecture and interiors during the Arts and Crafts period. Other than in context with the iconic log cabin, Rustic was not a historic revival style comparable to the others. In utilizing logs and irregular branches in its construction, Rustic was most popular for vacation homes and resort hotels. The term "Adirondack style" is sometimes used interchangeably with Rustic, and refers to the mountain range in New York where the style was first exploited for architecture of leisure. Widely employed on hotels and buildings in our national parks, the style has also been nicknamed "parkitecture." Despite the lack of any direct Arts and Crafts connection, the Rustic style remains aesthetically quite compatible. Now considered by some to be an integral part of the movement's revival, the Rustic influence makes a comfortable companion to the Craftsman style.

In the first decade of the twentieth century, the promise of a new century was still fresh, and the progressive designs of the Craftsman and Prairie styles were propelled

Figure 87.

House in San Rafael, California (c1910, with recent additions).

Recalling a stretched-out foursquare, this shingled home has the hipped (pyramidal) roof form and single central dormer most typical of that building type. In combination with simple enclosed eaves, the roof form also recalls the Prairie style. Recently added along two sides, a boldly scaled porch has pairs of substantial square columns in the Craftsman mode, set on low shingled walls interspersed with square-spindled railings. An octagonal porch corner extension adjoining the living room adds drama along with more outdoor living space. On the right side, the addition included excavation of basement-level space for a garage (partly seen), replacing a freestanding one that took up needed open space. On this corner site (not apparent in this view), the driveway connects to a street parallel to the home's right side. An original Colonial Revival accent, the tiny oval window is in a closet, which once had a sink, between two bedrooms. The same influence is seen in the original lozenge-shaped muntins in the upper sashes of first-floor windows partly visible on the porch. Common to the Colonial Revival, Shingle, and Craftsman styles are the gridded divided lights seen in the upper sashes of the second-floor windows. This example shows how various window styles can be successfully mixed.

Figure 88.

HOUSE IN SAN RAFAEL, CALIFORNIA (C1906, WITH RECENT ADDITIONS).

Predominantly Shingle style, this home also combines Craftsman and Colonial Revival elements. The main roof's gambrel form (not obvious in this view), matching the forward-facing gable on the right, is common to the Shingle and Colonial Revival styles. A trio of dormers, two with Craftsman-style shed roofs, helps break up the roof's mass. Between an angled bay window at left and the large gable, a recessed front porch is lined with tapering Craftsman columns, added in the recent remodel. Also in the Craftsman mode are the brackets (knee braces) attached to each column face to support open beamwork for vines. A welcoming entry and more porch privacy is created by a freestanding, wisteria-covered pergola spanning the front steps. Built of local stone, the retaining wall is an original feature. Added during the remodel, the gabled portion on the right shows typical Shingle-style detailing above its three upper windows. This new addition also incorporates a lower-level garage space, a family room and kitchen area adjoining the front porch, and an attic-level master bedroom. Despite these changes, the original home's character is essentially intact.

into sharper prominence. The public's interest in historicism had flagged, but only briefly. After World War I, public taste shifted towards the novelty of historic styles. By the 1920s, in a last gasp of eclecticism, these once again dominated the housing market, as the formerly progressive styles faded from fashion.

Colonial Revival Style

Ignited by America's centennial celebration in 1876, the public became steeped in feelings of patriotism and nationalism. The Colonial Revival movement was largely a product of nostalgia for the country's distant past. At the Centennial Exhibition in Philadelphia that year, many Americans got their first glimpses of antique artwork, furniture, and other artifacts dating to our country's earliest years. In a period rife with imported (and frequently overwrought) foreign styles, the event's attendees were impressed by the chaste purity seen in the displays of American art and artifacts

(continued on page 106)

Figure 89.

HOUSE IN SCITUATE, MASSACHUSETTS (C1910).

Dominated by the hipped (pyramidal) forms of its primary roof and first-floor porches, this home has elements of both the Colonial Revival and Craftsman styles. The shingled attic level dormers inventively adapt traditional gable forms; the one at left is bisected by the chimney. Most exterior walls are finished in unpainted "natural" stucco, a practical choice extolled by Gustav Stickley, which obviated the need and expense of repeated painting. Here paired with muted mossy green trim and cream-colored window sashes, the neutral color of stucco can harmonize with a variety of trim colors. A Colonial Revival trait, classical columns support the porch roofs. Not originally enclosed, the front porch now provides interior circulation and seating areas within its window-lined walls. French doors comprise the primary front entrance. The side porch on the left is only screen-enclosed and adjoins the living room. Shutters are also a Colonial Revival element and add places to apply trim color. Craftsman style is expressed in the exposed rafter tails, and in the brackets that support an overhang above the door at far right.

Figure 90.

LIVING ROOM IN THE SCITUATE HOUSE.

Despite its combination of exterior influences, this home's interior is a "textbook" example of Craftsman style. Suspended from intersecting box beams, original copper lanterns with obscured amber glass shades bear Gustav Stickley's mark. It has been speculated, but not yet conclusively proven, that this house may have been built or adapted from one of the "Craftsman" house plans sold by Stickley. From the enclosed front porch, entry to this room is through a secondary front door (out of view at right). In the far corner, a built-in bench at the foot of the stairs is detailed with slatted arms. Integral with the bench, a tall newel post is mounted with another original Stickley fixture. From the first stair landing, a door connects to the kitchen area. Behind the bench, a slatted screen shields the ascending stairs. On the same wall are a closet and built-in shelves. Through a doorway in the dining room at left, part of the kitchen is visible. Typical of this home's public rooms, high wainscot–paneled walls rise to a plate rail. Above it, a wallpaper frieze adapts a period design of stylized oak leaves and acorns. The carpet reproduces a pattern by British Arts and Crafts architect/designer C. F. A. Voysey.

Figure 91 (opposite).

DINING ROOM IN THE SCITUATE HOUSE.

With similarly crossing box beams, the dining room also retains its original copper lanterns by Gustav Stickley. Looking back through the same wide doorway seen in Figure 90, the living room fireplace is visible. Most of the doorway wall's thickness is created by the combined depth of built-in cabinets on either side. From floor to ceiling, the fireplace is faced with "tapestry brick," a period name given to this type of variable-colored brick, which presents a subtly shaded effect when assembled into an overall design. French doors on both sides of the fireplace lead to the screened side porch seen in Figure 89. Both rooms combine Arts and Crafts reproductions with period furnishings. The wallpaper frieze recreates a period landscape design of fir trees silhouetted against a subtle background of water and mountains.

(continued from page 102)
with classical influences, as well as the more primitive charm evoked by relics of our frontier settlers.

In the wake of the centennial, a growing interest in the historic architecture, interior design, and decorative arts of America's colonial past occurred across the country. Collecting American antiques emerged as a new obsession, and many such collections would later pass into our museums. At first, Colonial-inspired detailing was blended into other housing and furniture styles, but soon fully realized examples of the Colonial Revival began to appear. To some extent, it was a "purifying" force in American design. Foreign styles began to seem somehow misplaced and inappropriate. In this sense, the Colonial Revival can be considered as part of America's design reform movement. Instilled with a new sense of pride in our past, a reassessment of our own history was pivotal in the ongoing maturing of American culture.

Prior to World War I, the Colonial Revival style was more likely to be used as a crossover influence with the Shingle and Craftsman styles. After World War I, as the popularity of the earlier progressive styles faded, Colonial Revival expanded significantly. By the 1920s, it was more widely applied to architecture and interiors than ever, dominating American taste in decorating and furniture. Undiminished even by the advent of the Great Depression, the style continued to evolve even long after World War II. Remarkably, its shifting incarnations still managed to keep pace with evolving popular tastes. Today, the Colonial Revival style continues to survive and thrive as the longest-running domestic style in American history.

Colonial Revival Features

Among the easiest to identify, the Colonial Revival and its influence imparts a traditional feeling, and often one of greater formality. Depending on the scale and design of the house, the style was alternately used to evoke familiar quaintness, formal dignity, or pretentious grandeur. A design in this style or with its influence is signaled by the presence of classical-style elements derived from Greco-Roman antiquity. These adapt various forms and details observed on homes in the so-called Palladian or Georgian styles of America's eighteenth-century colonial period, which are primarily found in the eastern and southern states.

In their overall massing, most Colonial Revival homes are expressed as fairly simple volumes and are usually rectangular in plan. The most common roof forms are hipped (pyramidal), gabled, or combinations of these. Attic-level dormers were featured, and chimneys, usually of brick, were often placed as prominent design elements. Projecting porticoes (porches), both large and small, were common. Pediments (triangular gable-like forms, usually above doors and windows) also appeared. The façades of most Colonial Revival homes were symmetrical in composition. Variations occurred in examples designed to look as if they had been added to over a long period of time. Exterior walls usually feature narrow-width clapboard siding. Instead of brick for chimneys and foundations, some examples employ fieldstone, and on some, the exterior walls are also faced with stone.

Some application of classical elements usually occurs on both the interiors and exteriors of Colonial Revival homes, and the most typical of all are classical columns. Most often round but sometimes square, columns might be used in combination with matching pilasters (partial columns attached to a wall). The tops of

columns are terminated with capitals, which either copy or adapt one of the classical orders (i.e., Doric, Ionic, or Corinthian). Appearing in both single-story and monumental (two-story) versions, columns emphasized points of entry. Classical columns were also frequently employed to support open-beamed pergola structures, a popular crossover element often used with other styles, including Craftsman.

Both interior and exterior moldings are generally characterized by delicate complex profiles that also adapt traditional classical forms. To add interest to wider moldings, they might be reeded (fluted). Moldings with smaller ogee-type (double-curving) profiles may be used to frame wall panels, with larger versions used as crown moldings. Other common forms include "dentil" molding (with small, repeating cube-like squares) and "egg and dart" molding (with small arrow-shaped points set between ovoid forms, alternating in repeat). Most moldings were made of wood, and all were typically painted. Sometimes cast plaster was used instead for moldings or for other ornamental flourishes. Plaster moldings had profiles similar to those of wood. Used for both interior and exterior applications, other plaster elements included low-relief decorative panels (sometimes with figural scenes) used as accents, and friezes (of varying scale) that incorporated repeating patterns in wide borders comprised of Classical motifs such as wreaths, torches, ribbons, and swags.

An adjunct to Colonial Revival, related to the Spanish orientation of the next two styles discussed, is sometimes called Monterey Colonial. It was closely inspired by homes built by American settlers in Monterey (California) in the early nineteenth century, when that city was the Spanish Colonial regional capital. Originally employing adobe (mud brick) construction, these homes were often sheathed with wood siding. The most distinguishing feature is their distinctive second-floor balconies (sometimes extending around the house). These could be either cantilevered, or supported on posts from the ground. The balconies were covered by extended roof eaves, and also helped shade the first floor walls. Monterey Colonial was a sub-style among the primary 1920s historic revivals. Primarily built in California, its popularity persisted through the 1930s and 1940s. Often cited as this style's direct inspiration is the historic Larkin House (1835) in Monterey, which is open to the public as a house museum.

Mission Revival Style

The Mission Revival has been described as a Western equivalent of the Eastern Colonial Revival. This comparison is apt, considering the parallel that the Mission Revival also adapted forms of eighteenth-century buildings that occurred in colonial regions. Of course, the difference is that these regions were, at that time, colonial territories that belonged to Spain. The style name refers to the Franciscan missions that were built in various parts of the Southwest and served as religious centers for the conversion of Native Americans to Catholicism. In particular, the chain of twenty-one missions constructed in California (beginning in 1769 in San Diego) represented a major repository of surviving buildings from the Spanish Colonial era, although most had fallen into extreme disrepair by the late nineteenth century. At that time, a case was being made by the architectural community for the regional appropriateness of the Mission Revival as a building style for the West. While it came to be most favored and used there, examples of the style were also built across the country, far from any original missions.

The Mission Revival style was first favorably received at the 1893 World's Columbian Exposition in Chicago, where it was applied to California's exhibition

Figure 92.

HOUSE IN MINNEAPOLIS, MINNESOTA (1910).

Although less common in colder climates, this Mediterranean/Spanish—derived house shows that such designs were built far from the West or South. On a raised corner site overlooking a scenic urban lake, the house has white stucco walls and a red tile roof. Two primary living levels are ingeniously arranged into the hillside slope. Out of view toward the right, attached garages with servant's quarters above extend the building's overall depth, and are fronted by a drive-in entry court. With Arts and Crafts influence, casement (swinging) windows, which occur throughout, are stylishly divided by muntins with distinctive crossing linear and circular motifs. Probably the home's most striking exterior feature is its airy pergola, supported on classical columns and arranged into a sweeping curve that connects two short wings. Parallel to a curving window-lined wall of the dining room, the pergola shelters a spacious raised terrace. An early example, this anticipates the Spanish Colonial Revival designs that were so popular in the 1920s.

Figure 93.

HOUSE IN SAN DIEGO, CALIFORNIA (C1915).

Unless its story is known, it is not obvious that this "crossover" example of Mission Revival and Craftsman styles was originally designed around recycled building parts. Salvaged from a demolished, late-nineteenth-century commercial structure, the resurrected elements include the oversized arching windows, with unusual decorative spear-like elements applied to their crossing divisions, and the coiling wrought-iron balcony railing. In a Mission Revival detail that repeats the window arches, stucco walls rise into curving parapets and create solid railings for a pair of open sleeping porches. From the front corners, square pilasters rise like overgrown porch piers as bases for the wooden posts that support the hipped (pyramidal) roof. Like an abbreviated tower, a partly enclosed pavilion-like structure at the center has a slightly raised shingled roof. Its loggia (a covered porch, enclosed on three sides) extends to a semicircular balcony with the recycled railing. Exposed rafter tails occur in both Craftsman and Mission Revival designs. A recessed front porch at left balances the façade.

building. Also, the style's emergence was propelled by the overwhelming success of Helen Hunt Jackson's 1886 novel *Ramona,* which drew enormous attention to the history and romance of California's Spanish Colonial era. So it is not surprising to learn that it was in the spirit of promoting the Golden State for tourism and development that the Mission Revival style first appeared. It found favor in its earliest years as a style for commercial public buildings such as train stations, hotels, offices, retail stores, and apartment buildings. However after 1900, it was increasingly utilized as a style for private homes. Most often it was applied to larger homes, rather than modest bungalows.

The Mission Revival also had links to America's Arts and Crafts movement. Gustav Stickley made a visit to California in 1904, and then published an article in *The Craftsman* magazine about his experiences and observations there. He particularly admired the evocative ruins of the old missions, and was impressed by the simplicity and honesty of their thick adobe walls and rough timber-framed roof structures. In these, he saw American parallels to the tenets and ideals derived from medieval inspiration in the English Arts and Crafts movement that had already inspired his business. The plain, square-legged, rush-seated chairs that had once furnished the old missions have been cited as possible inspiration for so-called "Mission" furniture. That term also became a popular name for Stickley's Craftsman furniture (a name that he heartily disapproved of), and for its myriad generic look-alikes. It still persists in use by some today for that same furniture style.

Outwardly, the Mission Revival borrows detailing from the historic missions. Typical examples have red-tile roofs, usually hipped (pyramidal) in form, with deep overhanging eaves. Wooden structural details, some nearly identical to those in the Craftsman style (such as exposed rafter tails and brackets) are common. The Mission Revival's lifespan closely paralleled that of Craftsman, and the two were frequently combined in crossover examples. Gustav Stickley also published and sold Mission Revival–style house plans, and considered them entirely compatible with his other Craftsman designs. Notably, the interiors of earlier Mission Revival homes were sometimes designed entirely in the Craftsman style.

Gabled roofs (including peaked-roof dormers) are sometimes employed instead of (or in combination with) hipped forms. Gables are frequently detailed to include a parapet-like extension terminating in a scrolling (double-curved) simplified Baroque form across the top. This shape adapts that of a mission's *campanario,* a wide, (but shallow) flat-faced structure, pierced with a series of small arched top niches, built to house bells. In some grander Mission Revival examples, a tall, square bell tower may be included. Most of these rise a full story above the rest of the house, and were primarily for decorative effect. Usually such towers contain only a single upper room, which might be used as a bedroom, sleeping porch, or playroom.

Stucco-faced walls (usually white) are a basic feature of the Mission Revival style, and are often detailed to evoke the thickness of adobe construction. The use of rounded arches in repeating arcades that support shed-roof-covered porches is also characteristic. As with Craftsman, the style's prevalent window styles were both double-hung and casement types. In terms of today's remodeling issues, this style's simple materials are usually easy to match. While Mission Revival style continues to be interpreted today in new construction (most popularly in mild climate areas), few of these recent examples capture the sturdy simplicity expressed in the earlier versions. Despite its historic compatibility with the Craftsman style, most new versions tend to lack any visual references to it, an omission that certainly warrants reconsideration.

Spanish Colonial Revival Style

This later style developed as an outgrowth of the Mission Revival, and also adapted architectural forms brought from Spain to her New World colonies. Utilizing more complex elements of the more highly refined seventeenth- and eighteenth-century Spanish Baroque style, it was inspired mostly by designs and detailing of public buildings and churches. These examples of inspiration were primarily located in Central and South America, for most of North America's West (especially California) remained an unsettled, primitive wilderness for more than half of the eighteenth century. Although the Spanish Colonial Revival style was applied to homes both large and small, it was admired for very different reasons than the simpler Mission Revival, and garnered far fewer Craftsman-style associations.

The emergence of the Spanish Colonial Revival is closely linked to the buildings of San Diego's 1915 Panama-Pacific Exposition, held in the city's Balboa Park, which commemorated the opening of the Panama Canal. Designed by noted architect Bertram Grosvenor Goodhue (1869–1929), these buildings captivated the public with their rich detailing and romantic imagery. Although rendered in stucco, they were accented with Baroque-inspired sculptural ornament, an extravagant use of colorful glazed ceramic tile, and decorative wrought-iron embellishments. Such a lavish materials palette made the earlier Mission Revival style look downright austere by comparison. At this time, the public's growing preference for novelty historic styles was also a factor in its new popularity.

In the 1920s, the Spanish Colonial Revival style became one the most popular of all American housing styles, and it was applied to a great many bungalows. Some of its basic characteristics echo the Mission Revival, such as red-tile roofs, rounded arches, and stucco-finished walls (also usually white), but in overall forms and detailing there were considerable differences. The roofs are generally very shallow in pitch, typically without overhanging eaves, and may be hipped or gabled (or both). Some examples have courtyard plans, or include walled front gardens. Ornamental effects were widely used on both exterior and interior areas, and included accents of cast-plaster decoration. Glazed ceramic tile was often used on stair risers, in panels, and also on fountains (another common accent element). Curvilinear wrought-iron designs were common for window grilles, and stair or balcony railings. Window accents might also include turned-wood spindle screens, and sometimes leaded art-glass windows. Rambling, irregular compositions more typical of larger examples may include fancifully exotic features, such as rounded towers (sometimes with domes of glazed tile) or oversized parabolic-arched picture windows.

The Spanish Colonial Revival style persists as a viable choice for new construction today, and is most popular in areas with mild climates. Many today are discovering that both newer and vintage examples of this style make surprisingly sympathetic settings for Arts and Crafts furnishings and objects.

Figure 94.

HOUSE IN ALTADENA, CALIFORNIA (C1930).

This home has a Monterey Colonial influence, a mostly western regional style that was favored in California. Supported on extended beams rather than on posts or columns, the overhanging balcony is the style's most recognizable element. In this context, stucco walls evoke the sturdy informality of adobe. An Arts and Crafts sensibility is suggested by the simple expression of functional forms, seen in the original shutters with their "revealed construction" and working hardware, and in the detailing of the balcony's supporting beam-ends. Sited within private sprawling grounds, the home is complemented by several sympa-thetically styled outbuildings that create the feeling of a rural compound. Included among these is a detached garage with living quarters above (partly seen at far right), guesthouse, horse barn, and riding ring. During a major recent remodel, that was mostly applied to the interiors, the Craftsman-style influence was further cultivated and expressed.

Figure 95.

LIVING ROOM IN THE ALTADENA HOUSE.

Open to the entry hall through a wide arched opening, the home's main gathering space centers around its fireplace, which was redesigned as part of the remodel. A new handcrafted tile facing was adapted from period designs by Ernest Batchelder. Its shaded earthy colors have a matte finish, with accents of low-relief pictorial tile panels above and around the firebox opening. Cylindrical wall sconces in the Craftsman style match the paired lanterns of the ceiling fixtures. These are set off by a series of plain, square ceiling beams, which were added to bring more horizontal proportions and a cozier scale to the room. To the right of the fireplace, new built-in cabinetry includes a bench (with a lift-up seat) between tall open bookshelves. Recently crafted Arts and Crafts furnishings mix with Native American artifacts and period landscape paintings. Out of view is a doorway to the left that connects to a solarium (see Figure 96). In the entry hall, the turned spindle railing of the original staircase shows a traditional Colonial Revival influence. Less formal and more aligned with the Monterey Colonial style are the vertical paneling and detailing of the treads on the side of the staircase.

Figure 96.

SOLARIUM IN THE ALTADENA HOUSE.

This was originally an open-air patio area on the back of the house. The glass-covered structure already existed prior to the recent remodel, but was refurbished. Direct garden access is toward the right. A practical flooring material choice for an indoor/outdoor room, the irregular terra-cotta pavers are also style-appropriate for this house. Similar to the one seen on the front (in Figure 94), a second-floor balcony visible through the glass roof adjoins bedrooms. Because it also supports the solarium's heavy roof and framing, the balcony's cantilevered design needed more strength. It now rests on a beam that runs lengthwise, set on a series of square posts detailed with curving corbels. This structure provides additional design interest and effectively frames the fireplace. With a slightly irregular texture matching the stucco walls, the fireplace is accented with handmade tiles. Its distinctively stepped form creates multitiered display space for a diverse collection of tribal artifacts (many from New Guinea). The doorway at right connects to the living room, where the fireplace backs up to this one, and shares the same chimney.

Figure 97.

KITCHEN IN THE ALTADENA HOUSE.

The kitchen and breakfast room received a complete makeover that combined their previously separate spaces. Design cues were taken from the period kitchen of Greene & Greene's Gamble House in nearby Pasadena. The walls were faced with 3-inch by 6-inch white-glazed ceramic subway tile laid in the running bond pattern, which creates a durable washable surface that also brightens the space with its reflective finish. Also, in reference to the Gamble House kitchen, maple was employed for the flooring, woodwork, and cabinets. Because of its hardness and durability, it was a popular period choice for such utilitarian uses, and its warm, light color also has a pleasing aesthetic value. The recessed-panel detailing and wooden handles of the cabinets were also adapted from those in the Gamble House kitchen, as were the sugar pine countertops, which add a reddish accent amid the maple's golden tones. Cabinets with glass doors used on the upper areas line the breakfast room's far wall, adding useful counter and storage space. French doors open onto an intimate trellis-enclosed side garden area that features a lily pond.

BRITISH ANCESTRY

In the Tudor Revival & English Cottage Styles

Importing English Style

Before the influence of England on our early-twentieth-century homes, this country had long been influenced by British tastes. Even while at political odds with England for the first few decades of our independence, Americans sustained a reliance on popular British fashions. Although America's population was already ethnically diverse, the factors of a shared language and a lagging sense of our own cultural maturity helped encourage this situation. Besides architecture, interior design, and decorative arts, the British influence extended to our taste in the various fine arts as well.

By the dawn of the Victorian era (1837–1901), America was well on its way to establishing its cultural confidence. In matters of politics and commerce, the nineteenth century was the period when America matured into a world power. Yet, in terms of popular preferences in architecture and related design, Britain continued to hold sway until the last quarter of that century, when American taste began to be more established. Not surprisingly, this was after the 1876 Centennial Exhibition in Philadelphia, which kindled new interest in an American national identity and helped launch the Colonial Revival style.

During the first part of that same period, the Queen Anne style became dominant as America's most popular housing style. Despite its royal name, the style's potential Englishness was rather tenuously expressed, and it generally represented an almost completely American style. England's own equivalent, the Queen Anne Revival style, differed greatly. While some American examples did incorporate some recognizably English influences, it was mostly in their detailing. The majority had nary a visible trace amid their complexity. By the 1890s, the appearance of the restrained Colonial Revival style had already begun to replace America's taste for the flamboyant Queen Anne.

Importing a Movement: English Arts & Crafts

By 1900, something else was happening in America that was inspired by yet another British-born influence: Arts and Crafts. Initially, the colonization

(continued on page 119)

Figure 98.

HOUSE IN ROCHESTER, NEW YORK (C1928).

This appealing design in the East Avenue Preservation District was built by Howard Rupert for Henry H. and Mary Pease, and has been attributed to Syracuse architect Ward Wellington Ward. It skillfully arranges English-derived forms into an asymmetrical yet unified composition. Prominent roof areas are effectively highlighted by variously colored slate tiles. Tudor Revival–style half-timbering on the right is combined with a jerkin-headed (clipped) gable. Set into the peaked gabled portion on the left, a massive tapering stone chimney counterbalances the prominence of the right side, and seamlessly blends into matching stone on the shallow first-floor projection across the front. Expressed with its own roofline, this low stone portion helps impart a sense of modest scale appropriate to the home's predominant English Cottage style. Above the recessed front door, a gently arching rise in the roof adapts a similar thatched-roof detail that is not commonly rendered in slate. Matching stonework continues to the right on a low planter beneath a grouping of four windows.

Figure 99.

AINSLEY HOUSE, CAMPBELL, CALIFORNIA (1925).

Built for British immigrant J. C. Ainsley, this rendition of the English Cottage style was designed by A. M. Whiteside. It was moved to this location in Campbell's Civic Center from its original setting nearby and is now open to the public as a house museum. In 1884, Ainsley arrived in the Santa Clara Valley area, better known today as "Silicon Valley," which was then driven by an agricultural economy based on vast fruit orchards. Successful in the fruit-canning business, he specialized in exports to England, where California-grown varieties were popular. The stucco-faced house has retained its original "mock-thatch" roof, which arches rhythmically above each second-story window. At the center, a projecting "oriel" (small bay) window lights the main stair landing. To the left of the recessed front door is a large living room bay window, and to the right is the dining room. The bay at far right projects from the breakfast room (see Figure 102). Canvas awnings, often striped like those seen here, were common on various house styles of the 1920s.

Figure 100 (opposite).

ENTRY HALL IN THE AINSLEY HOUSE.

From the quartersawn oak-paneled entry hall, the view through the flattened "Tudor arch" doorway into the dining room extends into the breakfast room beyond. Windows and french doors throughout are divided by simple leaded grids like those seen at left. Above the arched doorways, finely hand-carved sprays of oak leaves and acorns adorn the narrow triangulated panels. Despite the home's calculatedly English flavor, the staircase's square newel posts and turned-spindle railing reflect Colonial Revival taste. Unusually configured, the stairway ascends to a mid-floor landing over the front door, directly above the outer recessed front vestibule, before turning to complete its rise. The window at the landing is also seen in Figure 99. This view is from another wide, arched doorway to the living room. The library (in Figure 101) is down a short hallway opposite the foot of the stairs. The home's well-preserved interiors retain the Ainsleys' original furnishings.

Figure 101.

LIBRARY IN THE AINSLEY HOUSE.

Dominated by the sweeping lines of a hand-hammered copper fireplace hood, this room has a more pronounced Arts and Crafts influence than any in the house. Its quartersawn oak paneling is similar to that of the entry hall. In a finely crafted detail, the recessed panels flanking the copper hood are gradually tapered in width to accommodate its flaring form. Streaked with blue-green patination along its riveted edges, the hood has a series of floral forms applied across the top. It rests on a pair of Batchelder tile corbels, which coordinate with the matte-finished tile surround in muted tones. More vividly glazed green and orange tiles occur on the raised hearth. Flanking the fireplace are built-in bookcases with simple leaded grids. Next to family photographs above them, a pair of lamps have ship motifs typical of the 1920s. The lounge chair and floor lamp are also characteristic of that decade. At a rear corner of the house, this room has windows on two sides, and enjoys pleasant garden outlooks.

Figure 102

BREAKFAST ROOM IN THE AINSLEY HOUSE.

Lined with windows, this cheerful room has a corner fireplace with its original gas heater insert. On the fireplace surround and hearth, ceramic tiles have mottled glazes and muted colors that show an Arts and Crafts influence. With a grapevine motif, a series of modular tiles around the opening creates a continuous meandering border design. Smaller tiles with bright floral forms accent the hearth. The original painted wall finish, a warm color with a subtly textured surface, has also been preserved. A close look at the woodwork moldings shows an "antiqued" painted finish similar to that of the breakfast room's dining set, which has hand-painted accents. Out of view at left is a double doorway to the dining room, which is fitted with french doors (seen in Figure 100). Through the doorway at right, an untouched period kitchen shows its original cabinets and white porcelain cast-iron sink, which has integral drainboards and matching legs typical of the era.

(continued from page 114)

of its ideas and practices reflected the English movement's tenets and ideals more directly. These were first forwarded most significantly by American proponents Gustav Stickley and Elbert Hubbard, who each founded his respective business on inspiration derived from firsthand visits to England, and with the movement's leaders there. However, American ingenuity soon led both men to adapt the movement to better suit our own cultural inclinations and business priorities. While only a few here perceived the English movement's aspect of socialistic idealism as realistic, its reverence for traditional craft skills and simplified design sensibility was more widely accepted, and these were the major English influences on America's version.

The architectural style component of the English Arts and Crafts movement had less of a direct translation here because it was expressed in far more limited ways in England than it would become in America. There, the movement's influence was most visibly demonstrated in large-scale, custom-built country homes of wealthy people, rather than in small middle-class dwellings comparable to American bungalows. This was a fundamental variation that reflected broader cultural differences. Here, the movement's aesthetic influence was far more broadly absorbed into the overall population. However, rather than being actively engaged in the movement's philosophy, most Americans who lived in environments influenced by it had little if any awareness of the movement, let alone its English sources. Once again, another influence of England had beset America, but this time its effect on public taste was largely due to manipulation by only a relatively few enlightened devotees who perceived the commercial potential of the Arts and Crafts movement on our shores.

Tudor Revival Style: Sources and Development

With its use of half-timbering as a visually defining element, the Tudor Revival is the most widely recognizable imported English style. Based on a system of structural timber framing employed on English and other European buildings of the medieval and early Renaissance periods, timbers used in the construction of the walls were left exposed. The spaces between were then filled with a mixture called daub, and given a finish coat of whitewashed plaster or stucco. Sometimes, mortared brick laid in patterns was used as infill. Outwardly, the resulting effect was the typical contrasting pattern of dark wooden beams set

Figure 103.

MUELLER HOUSE, MINNEAPOLIS, MINNESOTA (1912–1913).

Nestled in a tranquil wooded setting, this Lynnhurst area home is a crossover primarily of the Tudor Revival and Craftsman styles, but the prominent side-facing gables show Swiss Chalet influence in their bracketing, broad fascia boards, and vertical siding. On the left, an original sleeping porch extends into the trees. Craftsman detailing is seen in the deep eaves and exposed rafter tails, and in the treatment of the slightly overhanging second floor, which rests on a series of wooden corbels. The first floor's rough limestone-block facing makes a substantial base. Matching low stone walls on the open front porch and steps extend into the landscape. English influence is seen in the arched entry recess, where inset brick panels and leaded glass sidelights flank the front door. Above board-and-batten siding, long bands of windows recall Prairie-style placement. At right, a projecting half-timbered section with a front-facing gable (not visible) is supported by curving wooden brackets that rest on stone corbels. Paul Mueller, a landscape architect and civil engineer, designed this as his own residence. His wife, Ethel, was a noted portrait artist. The Muellers built this on a triple lot; they sold off their extra lots in 1925, moved the house about 100 feet, and also turned its street orientation in the process.

Figure 104.

STAIRCASE IN THE MUELLER HOUSE.

In the entry hall, the stairway parallels the front door. Its striking Craftsman-style detailing is immediately visible, and showcases the handcraftsmanship of its original assembly. With a detail more typical of the era's furniture, the wooden planks of the stair treads are mortised through the side stringers, where pairs of keyed tenons secure each one in place. Also in the Craftsman mode, closely spaced square spindles occur in the railings, and the turn of the stairs is anchored by gently tapering newel posts. The warm parchment color of the walls harmonizes with the oak woodwork. Other Arts and Crafts influence is seen in the hand-worked texture applied to the wall and ceiling plaster. To the left, a hall connects to the kitchen, and the door at right opens to the living room.

against a lighter-colored background. In the original models, the structural beams were also left exposed on the interior side of the walls. Somewhat ironic in an Arts and Crafts context, the half-timbering effects applied to nearly all of America's Tudor Revival homes are only thin boards—mere surface decoration that mimics the revealed construction of the historic examples.

The structural reference made by half-timbering is generally believed to be part of the original inspiration behind the linear "stick work" detailing that was applied to the exteriors of homes in the Stick (or Stick-Eastlake) style, beginning in the 1870s. But the most literal early evidence of Tudor Revival influence in America is traceable to some Queen Anne homes of the 1880s that included areas of half-timbered detailing. By the 1890s, some full-blown examples of Tudor Revival homes appeared, although initially, many of these derived their complex overall sense of massing from Queen Anne precedent. It was mostly after 1900, when the Arts and Crafts influence began to significantly affect American taste (mostly via the Craftsman style) that American examples of Tudor Revival influence were linked in any way to the movement.

The early leading proponents of the Arts and Crafts movement in America each acknowledged its English origins in prominent ways. For the Roycroft commu-

nity's campus in East Aurora, New York (founded in 1895), Elbert Hubbard chose to adapt the Tudor Revival as its thematic architectural style. In 1901, Gustav Stickley dedicated the first issue of his magazine *The Craftsman* to William Morris, the famous early leader of the English Arts and Crafts movement. Stickley also briefly sold furniture designed by architect/designer Harvey Ellis that featured metal inlays of typically attenuated English Arts and Crafts motifs. In the house designs and plans that Stickley marketed, simplified versions of half-timbering were routinely grafted onto otherwise Craftsman-style structures, and he was clearly comfortable with the crossover association that was implied. For a time, these initial links to America's Arts and Crafts movement created some public perception of its English influence, but this was never to become a mainstream association. However, it remains a fact that among the most seamless of any crossover designs occurring in the Craftsman-style context are those examples expressing a Tudor Revival influence.

Mostly in the higher-budget design world, the work of some American architects was influenced by the published projects of leading English Art and Crafts architects of its later phase, the generation that came after William Morris. Among these were M. H. Baillie Scott (1865–1945), Edwin Lutyens (1869–1944), and C. F. A. Voysey (1857–1941). Their skills were often more comprehensively applied to their

Figure 105 (opposite).

BAY WINDOW ALCOVE
IN THE MUELLER HOUSE.

One corner of the living room merges into an angled bay window alcove, which expands the spatial link to the dining room outward to capture garden views. Although it straddles the two rooms, the alcove retains its own identity, and is a pleasantly lit spot for reading. Below its casement windows, the angled sides are lined with built-in cabinets that create a useful open shelf on top. Expressing Prairie taste, original leaded art-glass transoms have geometric motifs suggesting small stylized trees. The patch of purple-painted ceiling marks one corner of the dining room. The color was lifted from a period-style border, which frames inset panels of green wallpaper with a vintage pattern of small leaves and berries flanking the alcove. The same treatment occurs in the panels of the dining room's high wainscoting (out of view). At left, built-in shelves abut the living room fireplace. To create more openness between areas, the wall is stepped down at its end, making a display shelf. Attractive and practical, the flooring of small, square terra-cotta tiles appears throughout the home's public spaces. Out of view in the center of the dining room, a shallow recess for a carpeting inset is surrounded by a tile border.

Figure 106.

BATHROOM DETAIL IN THE MUELLER HOUSE.

Located directly above the bay window alcove seen in Figure 105, this bathroom's outer window wall shares the same angled shape. The room's unexpected scheme of hand-sculpted and incised plaster decoration was created by Ethel Mueller, the original lady of the house, who was also an artist. Although such examples are not commonly found, the concept of ornamenting one's home with one's own handiwork is a quintessential Arts and Crafts ideal. From Quincy, Massachusetts, Mrs. Mueller adopted Minnesota as her home but missed the New England seaside. So, in the plaster above this bathroom's bay window, she incised a wistful poem about the sea. To complement the poem, she sculpted low-relief scenes of sailboats and seagulls on either side. Above the bathtub to the right, Ethel also created a large low-relief panel (partly visible) in which she incorporated stylized pine tree motifs—perhaps with Minnesota in mind—into a landscape scene. As part of a new paint scheme, the current owners recently had these unique decorations repaired and refreshed, adding a coordinated sponged finish on the lower walls.

projects, and extended beyond architecture to include the design of interiors and often their furnishings as well. Although there were some exceptions, such as Frank Lloyd Wright, this level of aesthetic control on residential projects was uncommon for most American architects in the early twentieth century.

After World War I, examples of the Tudor Revival were less likely to reflect the Craftsman crossover influence, and the style was more often perceived in the limited context of historic revivalism. An interest in greater historic authenticity accompanied the style into the 1920s, when Tudor Revival, along with English Cottage, became one of the most popular of any American housing styles. Although it was applied to variously sized houses, its prevailing popularity for the imposing homes of leading members of the business community earned it the nickname "Stockbroker Tudor."

Tudor Revival–Style Features

Often enhanced by their half-timbered detailing, the overall massing of Tudor Revival homes tended to have a vertical emphasis. Half-timbering commonly occurred on areas of the second floor, with the remaining walls usually faced with brick. To add a sense of character and age, larger Tudor Revival examples were fre-

quently designed to appear as if the house had been built in phases. Rooflines most typically employed steeply pitched gables with very shallow overhangs. Such roof forms displayed their covering prominently, and slate was considered the style's most desirable (and durable) roofing material. Fascia boards (bargeboards) were used to cover the angled eaves of gables, and might be accented with carved or pierced decoration. Large front porches were uncommon, and most front doors were instead sheltered by a small overhang or often set within a shallow recess.

It should be noted that many of the features assigned to Tudor Revival interiors were also found in examples of the English Cottage style, especially in larger ones. Even on more modest examples, the interiors of Tudor Revival homes usually expressed some aspect of their exterior style. In a rather literal example of this, a high-pitched gabled roof might be reflected on a home's interior as a vaulted (peaked) ceiling volume. This was likely to occur in a primary public area, usually the living room. Occasionally detailed with Gothic-inspired carving, beams might be applied to both flat and peaked ceiling configurations. Usually confined to grander examples, ornamental plasterwork that mirrored historic Tudor-period motifs ("strapwork" designs) was sometimes introduced on ceilings. Lighting styles tended

Figure 107.

HOUSE IN SEATTLE, WASHINGTON (C1915).

In the city's Capitol Hill area, this well-maintained house has a commanding presence and scale. The upper gable's half-timbering applies a Tudor Revival detail to a mostly Craftsman-style home. The asymmetrical sweep of the front gable displays handsome bracketing. Above the porch, a small-scale angled bay with multipaned windows, called an "oriel" in the English context, has a shed roof. Unpainted natural stucco, a practical Craftsman-era favorite, faces the upper two levels. The pronounced division between floors contributes more horizontality to this somewhat vertical design. Most of the color here is supplied by the earthy red-brown brick that faces the first-floor walls and anchors the house. Brick is also used for the massive square columns of the front porch, which support enormous structural beams. Their scale is offset by the arching form of the crossbeam. Above it, a series of exposed rafter tails with shaped ends project in the manner of a pergola. Curves repeat in the arched tops of triple windows (with transoms) on either side. The brick extends to a low wall around an open front terrace, with a partial-height column on the left, and is continued on either side of the front stairs. A recent addition, the low brick wall in the foreground adapts the same form and detailing seen around the brick terrace. Arching ironwork between the posts echoes the façade's curving elements.

Figure 108 (opposite).

COSTELLO HOUSE, PORTLAND, OREGON (1911).

Noted local architect Joseph Jacobberger designed this corner home in the historic Irvington district for James and Mary Costello. It was recently restored to its original appearance. Sophisticated in design, an influence of the (post-Tudor) Jacobean style is seen in the small pair of gables, detailed without any overhanging eaves, on the façade's right side. As such, they seem to be, in equal measure, expressions of both the front wall and the roof. On the left side, inspiration from English Arts and Crafts architecture occurs in the other gable and roof forms, small hipped-roof dormer, and angled bay (oriel) window. The irregular stone facing on the first floor and chimney unifies the composition. Not a full story, the stone's suppressed height gives emphasis to the large first-floor windows extending above, and to other features of the second floor and roof. Simple detailing and square stone columns on the open side porch show both Prairie and Craftsman influence. Tethered by chains to the eaves above, the curved iron-and-glass canopy over the front door is among the home's distinctive and elegant features.

to express spiky or pierced metal, Gothic-inspired motifs, but brass fixtures with later bulbous, English Baroque-inspired forms were also popular. If a central chandelier appeared in primary public rooms, it was usually accompanied by one or more sets of matching wall sconces.

A feature of English origin shared with Craftsman-style interiors was a fireplace set into an alcove called an inglenook, where it was typically flanked by built-in benches. Fireplaces often incorporated tall, tapering chimney enclosures that resembled hoods (SEE FIGURE 112). Some mantels were made of wood, which might include decorative carving, but stone (or cast stone) was often employed. Commonly, a flattened version of the pointed Gothic arch, called a "Tudor arch," was applied to fireplace openings. It was also a favorite shape for the front door, which often featured sets of wrought-iron hardware, including long, decorative strap hinges. The Tudor arch was sometimes extended to other interior doors and to wide doorway openings. A period English woodcarving motif, the "linenfold" pattern made an authentic statement when applied to wall paneling, which in some cases only occurred on one wall.

In larger examples, staircases were made into prominent design elements, and most were detailed with substantial turned wood spindles. It was popular to light two-story stairwells with oversized windows that might incorporate some leaded art-glass designs, although sometimes only clear glass was used within the leaded pattern. In some earlier versions of the Tudor Revival style, including Craftsman crossovers, windows were double-hung (vertically sliding) and divided into diamond-shaped panes by wood muntins (usually only in the upper sash). In other examples, casement (swinging) windows were more likely to feature diamond-paned leading, sometimes inset with colored-glass accents. Combinations of both double-hung and casement windows also occur in some homes of this style.

English Cottage Style: Sources and Development

In evaluating the English Cottage style in historical terms, it is important to realize that its vernacular meaning was modified in early-twentieth-century America to suit our house-marketing purposes. In Great Britain, "English cottage" refers to a tradi-

Figure 109.

FOREST HILL CLUB HOUSE,
SAN FRANCISCO, CALIFORNIA (1919).

Framed by a twisting cypress tree, this building was designed by the important and progressive Bay Area architect Bernard Maybeck (1862–1957). With a prevailing Arts and Crafts sensibility, he incorporated Tudor Revival elements that include half-timbering, scalloped fascia boards and steeply pitched gabled roofs into its multi-layered composition. Distinctly separate parts that vary in detailing and materials are arranged as if they may have evolved over time. Existing paint colors are based on site investigations, which determined Maybeck's original scheme. Although a caretaker's living quarters occupy the gabled portion on the left, this is not a house. Originally commissioned by the Forest Hill Association as a neighborhood amenity with multiple uses, it was conceived to help attract prospective homeowners to the developing area. Its siting in the midst of this upscale residential enclave dictated a compatible scale and style. At the inside corner of the L-shaped structure, a wide front door leads to a low-ceilinged entry hall, opening to a dramatic, peaked-roof room in the right-hand wing. With an oversized fireplace on the far right wall, there is also a partial open loft area above this main room toward the rear. The atmospheric club house is accessible to the public as a venue for special events (see Resources, page 190).

tional, but broadly generic, house category. Generally, they are homes in rural settings, many built as farmhouses, often with traditional thatched roofs. The farmhouse precedent also suggests these are homes of relatively modest scale. Most were built simply, and of locally found materials. Generally, the overall form, construction, and detailing of "true" English cottages was determined by the established building traditions of their particular region of that country.

In America, the Tudor Revival was the earlier of the two English-derived styles to appear in its early-twentieth-century houses, largely because of an initial association with the Craftsman style. Although it was an adaptable style in terms of scale, Tudor Revival was most favored for larger two-story homes. At the same time, when Tudor Revival was applied to smaller bungalows, the term "English Cottage" sounded more appropriate, and thus its use became common to connote modest scale.

After World War I, more plan book designs were described as English Cottage homes, and their popularity helped to further define the characteristics that became established features of the style. Ensuring success and high visibility, the English Cottage style found its most significant niche in the bungalow marketplace. Even after it had secured its own identity, it was sometimes combined with Tudor Revival detailing, which tended to occur more often on larger-scale examples (SEE FIGURE 98). Not limited to any particular region of the country, the English Cottage style became one of America's most popular housing styles during the 1920s.

English Cottage–Style Features

In contrast to the conspicuous presence of most Tudor Revival homes, English Cottage–style examples exude a less formal and more understated presence, a reason why it was especially appealing for bungalows. However, the style was occasionally applied to larger homes with some success (SEE FIGURES 98–99). Separate from their scale, homes in the English Cottage style are usually most defined by the form of their roof. One of the most popular ways to evoke the style was to detail the roof with "jerkin-headed" (clipped) gables, which appear as if their gable peaks were sliced off at a 45-degree angle (SEE FIGURE 98). A traditional European roof framing detail, it was not exclusively English-derived, but in America it developed an English Cottage association. Especially when applied to a single-story house, clipped gables also make the house appear somewhat lower and smaller.

While slate roofs were expensive, they mirrored the traditional roofing material of many actual examples of historic stone cottages in England's Cotswold region, and sometimes slate also appeared on homes of modest scale in America. Because it is very heavy, slate is most likely to be used on roofs with eaves of minimal depth. Another traditional English roofing material was terra-cotta tiles, which were cut and hung over wood framing much like wooden shingles, but were far more durable. Some terra-cotta tiles were shaped as interlocking forms for a tighter fit. However, this treatment was not particularly common with English Cottage–style homes in America. Considering its comparable expense, slate was a more popular option.

Another undeniable expression of the English Cottage style was evoked by homes detailed with "mock-thatch" roofs (SEE FIGURE 99). Usually an attention-getting novelty feature, this improbable treatment occurred most often in the 1920s. Using wooden shingles, architects sought to re-create the rounded form and thick-

ened eaves of an actual thatched roof. Numerous examples of so-called "storybook-style" homes—an overtly picturesque sub-style of the English Cottage—employed mock-thatch roof detailing. Novelty and quaintness had sales appeal, and guided the application of such roofs to otherwise more conventional-looking homes, including numerous plan book designs.

The process of constructing a mock-thatch roof was quite labor intensive, and for this reason, it was never really commonplace. To achieve the effect, the structure of the gable peaks and eaves were modified to create a dimensional roundness over which the wooden shingles were applied. These required hand cutting, and were meticulously fitted into undulating courses of irregular width, which at the curving outer edges required them to be individually steam-bent. Many such roofs have held up remarkably well over the years. In some cases, the wood shingling was replaced with inexpensive composition shingles, and the overall effect is diminished. The expense of replacing mock-thatch roofs exactly as they were built is an extremely costly undertaking. Although a highly skilled roofing contractor could re-create one, mock-thatch roofs are rarely attempted on homes of new construction, and remain a fanciful anachronism.

Other characteristic features of the English Cottage style included the use of leaded diamond-paned windows, most typically on the casement (swinging) type. Colored art glass was less commonly seen. In warmer climates, the exterior walls were likely to be finished in painted stucco. In colder locations, brick was usually employed, with many color and textural effects available with that material. While stone walls do have an English historic precedent with cottages, these were not usually applied to smaller-scale homes. However, some designs utilized stone chimneys, foundations, and partial stone walls as effective accents (SEE FIGURE 98).

It should be noted again that many of the same interior elements previously described in the context of Tudor Revival homes also often appeared in examples of the English Cottage style, and therefore don't require extensive repetition here. While the grander interior elements of Tudor Revival homes would more likely occur in larger-scale examples of the English Cottage style, the same characteristic, and sometimes Gothic-inspired, forms and details were commonly applied to various interior features of both these styles (doors, woodwork, windows, fireplaces, etc.) as convenient ways to reinforce their "English" character. As with Tudor Revival, any pronounced Craftsman influence was most likely to occur on the interiors of English Cottage examples built prior to World War I.

As their distant historic background associations would suggest, existing vintage examples of America's English Cottage style, as well as those of the Tudor Revival, tend to look their best when they convincingly impart a feeling of age or "character," not shabbiness. Certainly a setting of mature landscaping can help to suggest an established sense of permanence for any historic revival home. Yet, our English Cottage–style homes remain essentially fanciful attempts at re-creating a historic past that is only fiction in America. The style is not commonly considered in the context of new construction today, and most attempts at instantly achieving any plausible historic English cottage character are now seldom effectively achieved. For those who love this or most of the other historic revival styles, restoring or renovating a surviving vintage example remains the most promising option.

Figure 110.

HOUSE IN SAN FRANCISCO, CALIFORNIA (c1920).

A rambling assemblage of different volumes, this English-inspired home combines steeply pitched, gabled forms with a hipped (pyramidal) roof near its center. The plan of the interior is equally varied, with multiple level changes that pack a lot of living area into a relatively small urban footprint. The home's most dominant exterior element is the peaked section at right, containing the living room (see Figures 111 and 112). With influence borrowed from grander examples of English Arts and Crafts homes that were widely published at the time, the soaring height of the projecting bay and the room's other tall windows add considerable distinction. Otherwise minimal in detail, the exterior does include some half-timbering (out of view) in the gable of a two-story section on the far left that includes the garage. On a corner site with a slight uphill rise, the recently landscaped house is approached diagonally by an irregular flagstone path. Brick stairs lead to a raised open terrace enclosed by low stucco walls, creating usable outdoor living space. Partly obscured, the recessed front door is located within the smallest gabled portion at center.

Figure 111 (above).

LIVING ROOM IN THE SAN FRANCISCO HOUSE.

From a low-ceilinged entry hall toward the right, the living room opens up into a dra-
matic volume of space and light. To either side, the ceiling reflects the angle of the roof
pitch, while toward its center, the peak is "clipped" into a flat plane. Resting on curving
corbels, pairs of angled beams follow the ceiling configuration. The tall windows are
divided into a series of panels, including some openable casements along the bottom row.
Of mostly clear glass, they are simply divided by a series of slightly wavy leaded lines,
intended to imply a feeling of age. In the upper rows, the top of each window forms a
flattened "Tudor arch," lending some Gothic character. Another fanciful historic refer-
ence is made by the colored art-glass motifs of stylized heraldic shields set within circular
frames, which repeat in all the upper windows. A mélange of Arts and Crafts and other
styles, the furnishings mix period pieces with reproductions. The area rug and chair
upholstery at right adapt English Arts and Crafts period textile designs by William Morris.

Figure 112 (opposite).

LIVING ROOM (TOWARD DINING ROOM)
IN THE SAN FRANCISCO HOUSE.

In this view, the living room is seen from the direction of the corner shown in Figure 111. The wide Tudor
arch-topped dining room doorway matches one to the entry hall (out of view, toward the left). Centered at
the far end of the room, the original cast-stone mantel was made to resemble limestone. It features low-
relief ornament in the English Renaissance style, and its opening repeats the Tudor-arch form. Combined
with the bold verticality of its tapering chimney, the fireplace design exploits the room's height. Such hood-
like forms were favored for Tudor Revival fireplaces. Partly seen, the dining room features a room-wide,
bow-shaped bay lined with all-wood casement (swinging) windows, with muntins arranged in simple grids.
Partially visible beyond the dining room's ceiling fixture is a recessed alcove with a freestanding sideboard, a
design feature that saves floor space. As was also true with the other historic revival styles popular in the
1920s, the built-in furniture typical of earlier Craftsman interiors had by then become less fashionable.

Figure 113 (opposite).

KITCHEN IN THE SAN FRANCISCO HOUSE.

With successful results, this recently remodeled kitchen interprets the Craftsman style, which complements (but doesn't compete with) the home's English character. The space was reconfigured to be more open. In the far corner, a swinging door to the dining room is next to a pocket door to the entry hall. Quartersawn oak was employed for the cabinetry throughout. Although few period kitchens sported the refined finishes seen here, most did employ similarly basic, recessed-panel cabinet doors and flush-front drawer units. Appropriate for the home's character, the profile of the crown molding above the cabinets continues around the room, making a traditional and unifying statement. To offset the preponderance of wood, handcrafted tile with a blue-green glaze was chosen for both the countertop and backsplash areas. Further design interest is added by matching narrow tile borders with low-relief decoration, as well as a panel with a stylized oak tree seen above the range. Expanding the compact breakfast area is an angled bay with a built-in window seat, with fabric that adapts a vintage William Morris pattern. Out of view at the room's opposite end is a door to the garden, and stair access to the laundry room, and basement level.

Figure 114.

FAMILY ROOM IN THE SAN FRANCISCO HOUSE.

Situated directly beneath the living room, this is part of a well-lit, mostly above-ground base-ment that includes a guest bedroom, bathroom, secondary kitchen (for entertaining), and extensive storage space. A lower ceiling height determined the horizontal proportions of the room, which has its original Craftsman-style fireplace. Built of clinker brick, the design shows off that material's irregular textural effects and deeply shaded coloring. In an abbreviated ver-sion of the tapering hood-like form of the living room fireplace, the brick extends to the ceiling. The arched opening is set between a pair of tapered pilasters. Below the mantel, a section of contrasting red bricks incorporates some stepped corbelling and a row of square and rectangular recesses. Some handcrafted blue-green, matte-glazed tiles are temporarily propped within the recesses while the owners decide whether the tiles should become permanently-installed accents. The bookcases at left were added, but the built-in bench by the fireplace is an original feature.

◼

CASE STUDIES

Closer Looks at Vintage Home Remodels

On Making Changes

Selected as "case studies," each of the examples in this chapter are period homes that were recently subject to a significant remodeling. Although their outward appearances vary widely, all of them included some kind of new addition as part of their renovation project. They are spotlighted here so that their most significant attributes can be understood and appreciated. Each can be a source of learning useful design lessons and an inspiration for new ideas. Because these homes illustrate various attitudes and approaches to the design process of their remodel, their wide variety of solutions reflects a diversity of personal taste. What they have in common is that each of the projects has both respected and enhanced the design integrity of the original house.

In the context of historic preservation, the remodeling of period homes can be a sensitive issue. Some people stand by the belief that, in general, historic houses should be maintained or restored as closely as possible to their original condition. While there is a simple nobility to such a conviction, it usually reflects more idealism than reality, and isn't a realistic attitude that can be universally applied.

Important exceptions to this are house museums, which are used as learning tools, and specifically meant to interpret their own original history, design, and period for the benefit of the public's education and enjoyment. In most such cases, there are official and specific historic preservation guidelines already in place, and these must be closely followed. Otherwise, critical issues concerning funding sources and tax credits may be in jeopardy. As part of the public domain, America's historic house museums are among our most precious resources. Each deserves whatever reverence, respect, and financial assistance their communities and their visitors can generate for them.

There are degrees of exception to the strictest interpretations of approach to the stewardship of historic

(continued on page 138)

Figure 115.

HOUSE IN SAN FRANCISCO,
CALIFORNIA (C1920S, WITH RECENT ADDITIONS).

Covering much of its urban lot in the Forest Hill neighborhood, this home's steeply pitched roof and half-timbered gable ends primarily imply Tudor Revival as a design influence. However, its rounded tower and conical roof are forms more characteristic of medieval French buildings. The design typifies the prevailing eclectic taste of the 1920s taste for historic revival styles or crossover combinations. Both its steep roofline and tower also bear comparison to the example seen in Figure 146, which dates from the same period. But this home is not (at least outwardly) what it appears. Most of the parts that are visible from the street were recently constructed, as part of a major remodel of an existing vintage house. It had the same basic wall and window configurations seen in this view, except for the addition of the tower. This was part of major changes made to create a more dramatic roofline, which previously had only jerkin-headed (clipped) gables. The original windows were precisely reproduced, but all the half-timbering and bracketed detailing are newly added features. A consideration in undertaking such a significant makeover was the visibility of its uphill siting, which helped prompt this stronger style statement. The surrounding area's precedent of other surviving period homes, in similarly picturesque styles, was helpful in conceiving the new design. Now the remodeled house makes a far more effective design statement, yet blends into its streetscape as if it had always looked like this.

Figure 117 (above).

APPROACH TO THE BOETTCHER MANSION.

In contrast to the portion with walls built entirely of stone as seen in Figure 116, the adjoining wing of the house at left employs the same stone for its foundation level only. The stucco-faced upper walls are divided by natural tree trunks, now painted, which were peeled of their bark and applied in the manner of half-timbering. This indirect English reference is echoed in the use of clipped (jerkin-headed) gables on the home, including its attic-level dormers. Linked to the house by an open gateway is the original garage, a matching but much smaller structure partly seen at right. Openings that once admitted cars have been filled in with french doors, and its first-floor interior is now a single assembly space. Beyond the gateway, a walkway lined with an appropriately informed garden leads to the home's remodeled front entrance. Marked by an attached pergola and comprised of a recent addition, it contains a new reception hall (see Figure 118). This change has improved access for the visiting public, and also better serves the building's requirements as an events venue.

Figure 118 (opposite).

RECEPTION HALL IN THE BOETTCHER MANSION.

Originally an outdoor U-shaped entry court, this two-story space was created by its enclosure, and blends well into the existing structure (see Figure 117). Glimpsed at upper right is a dormer window in the new roof. An opening at upper left was previously an outside window in a second-floor hallway. Out of view, the wall on the left that once enclosed the second-floor stair hall was removed, creating an open loft-like space that overlooks the room. To buffer the elements, entry from outside is first through a window-lined vestibule. On either side of its inner french doors (partly seen at right) are double-hung, multipaned windows providing more daylight. A series of painted flat moldings encircling the room temper its vertical proportions. Craftsman-style wall sconces set into narrow painted panels match the central chandelier. Articulating different wall levels, the moldings allow for separately painted and wallpapered areas. On the lower walls is a re-created Arts and Crafts–period pattern by William Morris. A vintage Walter Crane design is adapted in a wide frieze with a woodland animal motif, whose matching border at the top sets off the rose-colored painted wall area in between. Most of the furnishings replicate authentic Craftsman pieces.

Figure 116.

THE BOETTCHER MANSION, GOLDEN, COLORADO (1917).

This home expresses mostly the Rustic and Craftsman styles. Sited on Lookout Mountain, it was built as a summer home and hunting lodge for Charles Boettcher, a successful Denver-based German emigrant. His "castle in the clouds" was designed by Fisher and Fisher, a prominent architectural firm of that city. Three successive generations of the Boettcher family enjoyed use of the property. Expressive of its natural setting, irregularly sized boulders of local stone were used for the rugged walls of this portion, which contains an enormous living room with a peaked ceiling. On the projecting entry vestibule is a clipped (jerkin-headed) roof gable recalling the English Cottage style. The original arched front door, which has long strap hinges, is glimpsed in its recess. With panoramic views, a spacious, raised open terrace is surrounded by low walls of matching stone. A single-story sun porch, adjoining one end of the living room, is partly seen at right. First built as part of the open terrace, the sun porch was shaded by an open-beamed pergola with massive stone columns, which later were incorporated into its enclosing walls. Another matching sun porch (out of view to the left) is at the opposite end of the living room. The Boettcher Mansion is open to the public for tours, and as a venue for special events (see Resources, page 189).

(continued from page 134)
buildings that can apply to period homes in designated historic districts. In that context, preserving a home's original outward appearance is especially important for maintaining its representative nature in context with its historic neighborhood. Usually generated on a local level, official guidelines also determine what can and cannot be done to the exteriors of homes in such areas—not that every homeowner will necessarily agree with them. But most owners of historic district homes find their neighborhood's special status to be a positive factor, and it generally tends to enhance property values in the vicinity. However, it is notable that the interiors of homes in designated historic districts are not protected from inappropriate remodeling (such as the removal of original features). So the education of its homeowners about their importance is therefore a critical task for local preservationists to achieve.

Some owners of historic houses may not be aware of the Mills Act, which can provide significant tax breaks on expenses incurred by restoration projects. This can, in effect, help subsidize some of the costs that are often unexpected or overwhelming to homeowners committed to preserving their vintage homes. While the Mills Act may not apply to every project, it is well worth the effort to investigate its requirements before proceeding with any new work.

Tread with Caution

In considering the bigger picture, the greatest numbers of old house owners are not bound by too many rules and restrictions other than those governed by the local building codes. While for many this freedom is quintessentially American, it can be both a blessing and a curse for vintage houses and older neighborhoods. Since each area has its own unique housing stock and particular issues of concern, it is not possible here to attempt to define, in any general fashion, what may or may not be right or wrong to do to a vintage house. What can be unequivocally stated is that old houses should be treated with the respect they have earned by their survival. In considering making changes to an old house, a reasonable degree of education about its own history, as well as its style and period, should occur before any action is initiated. While qualifying such a subjective pronouncement is elusive, it can suffice instead to say, "Tread with caution."

The inherent implication in the term "case studies" applied to houses in this chapter is that each should represent some innovative design solutions to common problems, and offer some transferable inspiration through their examples. The

Figure 119.

LIVING ROOM INGLENOOK IN THE BOETTCHER MANSION.

With an arching form, the inglenook is well integrated into this room's irregular stone walls. Recalling a medieval great hall, the living room has an impressively peaked ceiling; its structural beams (partly seen at upper left) are exposed. Replacements of lost originals, the cylindrical Craftsman-style lanterns hang from projecting beam-ends along each side wall. An arch-topped fireplace opening echoes the inglenook's form. A pair of stone corbels with angled fronts and shield-motif embellishments support a thick oak mantel shelf. Previously missing, a pair of freestanding benches was exactly reproduced from a period photograph. They are sturdily constructed of solid oak planks, with their seats mortised through the curving side panels, and their tenons secured by pairs of oversized keys. For greater comfort, the bench backs are slightly angled. Throw pillows reproduce Arts and Crafts—period designs. As an events venue, this oversized room comprises the building's main gathering space, so is kept mostly unfurnished to maximize its flexibility.

example of the Boettcher Mansion (see Figures 116–119) is unique for this chapter because it is open to the public. Not a house museum in the strictest sense, it doubles as a special events venue, which largely funds its own operating and maintenance costs. Since its recent changes were made to enhance its present use, they must be considered in that context. All the rest are private homes, lived in and loved by the owners who implemented the changes presented. While some took a quieter path of design restraint, mostly inspired by historic authenticity, others are more boldly inventive with a contemporary edge. It is fascinating to make comparisons between the choices made for each home. However, they are each presented objectively, and stand on their own merits. Ultimately, evaluating the extent of their success is a subjective pursuit for the reader to enjoy pondering.

As Good as New

Everyone involved in the following projects would most likely concur that the verdict is still out on whether tackling a major old house restoration or renovation project is more complex and all-consuming than building a new house. Whichever direction

Figure 120.

HOUSE IN LOS ALTOS, CALIFORNIA (1915).

Originally built for John B. Shenk, a California Supreme Court Justice, this Craftsman-style home's recent major renovation included a significant rear addition, entirely redesigned landscaping, and extensive interior work throughout. Sited on three city lots, it has 200 feet of gently curving street frontage that was previously enclosed by chain-link fencing and overgrown hedges, which blocked views of both yard and house from the street. Shifted from its former alignment with an offset front door, the entrance is now at the lot's center. A low front gate of arching form with strap hinges and slatted detailing is set within a lantern-hung entry pergola. The stone-and-brick masonry style of the tapering piers matches the adjacent posts and low walls below the board-and-batten wood fencing. Softly rounded like a handrail, the fence's solid wooden cap also has subtle "cloud lift" detailing, inspired by the work of Greene & Greene. Its height permits passersby to enjoy views of the front garden. In another street-friendly gesture, the front fence jogs in and out, running parallel to the house rather than the curving street. This creates street-side planting pockets at balanced intervals along the fence's length, that soften its impact and break up its mass.

is chosen, then, shouldn't be determined by any perception of greater ease or speed. The following examples show the adaptability of old houses to incorporate various new features desired by their owners. They also prove that building from scratch certainly isn't the only route to acquiring one's own dream house.

As survivors of another era, old houses offer tantalizingly physical glimpses into a past that can otherwise only be imagined. But simply being a surviving vintage home, or even a superior example of a historic style and period, shouldn't necessarily dictate everything about how a house is lived in, maintained, improved, or possibly enlarged. With proper care, old homes can survive indefinitely. But, like people, houses change. And, as houses get older, they tend to need more help to look their best, and to keep working properly. While they may not necessarily live forever, old homes can provide ways for us to connect with our past, and also participate in our future.

Figure 121.

FRONT OF THE LOS ALTOS HOUSE.

On axis with the relocated front entry gate (seen in Figure 120), a circular fountain (at lower left) is at the center of a welcoming and open, paved courtyard-like area. With muted color from a transparent greenish stain, the home's shingled walls have a subtly textured surface. Unchanged in this view, original Craftsman-style features include a multi-gabled roof, deep over-hangs, exposed rafter tails, oversized brackets (knee braces), and a shed-roof dormer. In the surviving original masonry treatment, clinker brick with ran-dom river rock accents is employed alongside the front steps, and for the low railing wall around the full-width front porch where the new front door (Figure 126) is partly seen. The railing wall's broad concrete caps may be used for occasional seating or for potted plants. These original areas served as convenient models for new masonry for the veranda and terrace areas that were added onto the sides and back (see Figures 123 and 124). For masonry work not directly attached to the house (see Figures 120, 122, and 125) in various garden areas, this treatment was not precisely copied, but historic precedent from elsewhere provided the inspiration for its mix of similar mate-rials. Outside stairway access to the basement level is on the right side.

Figure 122 (left).

FRONT GARDEN OF THE LOS ALTOS HOUSE.

Although partly obscured by trees, the house is seen along with its garden areas that occur inside the front fence (seen in Figure 120). Unlike the more pri-vate garden spaces, this is formally organized, and was inspired by the garden planning of grand English Arts and Crafts country homes. Adjacent to the front steps and gabled porch are the entry courtyard area and circular foun-tain (also seen in Figure 121). With a red glazed ceramic pot for its quietly overflowing water source, the fountain is at the center of the long, shallowly proportioned front yard area, which is now organized into an axially aligned sequence of "outdoor rooms" to either side. Framing views and defining each of these areas, tapering posts of brick and stone are attached to low bench-height walls. Counterpoints to the fountain, a pair of large planted ceramic urns to either side are set on circular brick plinths (bases), and each marks the center of the adjoining areas. At the far end, serendipity allowed a huge speci-men deodar cedar tree to be centered in its own "room," which corresponds to an open seating area at the opposite end (out of view) that completes this balanced sequence of front garden spaces. Irregular flagstone paving set in low ground covering injects an informal note and blends the adjacent areas.

Figure 123 (right).

SIDE VIEW OF THE LOS ALTOS HOUSE.

The large gabled portion at far left shows the home's original depth. The new addition extends back and makes an L-shaped right turn toward the garage. An open terrace, detailed to match the masonry of the front porch (see Figure 121), bridges a single-story hipped-roof bay of the dining room with the addition, which contains the new kitchen, family room, and second-floor master bedroom with the open balcony. Where the building turns, a door opens to a hall connecting the kitchen, laundry room, and garage. Stairs lead from the hall to an art studio and bathroom on a partial second floor over the garage. The first-floor shed-roof detailing on the garage helps reduce its mass. Both this and the opposite side garden are screened from the front areas and street by a wood lattice-topped privacy fence (glimpsed in Figures 121 and 124). Irregular flagstone paving is set into the grass to define free-form lawn areas, and also extends around a birdbath. Raised on a brick base, the birdbath was made by pairing a shallow copper basin with an inverted, flaring ceramic pot. Its alignment with the terrace steps and central placement makes this area's only formal gesture.

Figure 124 (left).

SIDE AND REAR VIEW OF THE LOS ALTOS HOUSE.

This rear corner of the new addition is wrapped by a roomy veranda (see Figure 127) whose details were copied from the front porch. These include a roof outlined by copper gutters, a gable over the stairs at right, paired posts, and the masonry treatment. Out of view at left is a fireplace in an "outdoor room" (seen in Figure 125) that aligns with the steps on the left. Variations in height and forms on the addition's roof help break up its mass. All of its detailing is adapted from the home's original portion (out of view). At the far left, the garage's second floor is partly seen. The three horizontal windows in the upper rear gable are in the master bedroom, and windows to the master bath are seen in the smaller gable at right. At its left end, the veranda opens to the kitchen area through a two-piece "Dutch door." Through french doors on the right, the family room at the corner also opens to the veranda. At its far right end, there are french doors to the parlor adjoining the living room. The side garden is screened from the front by a lattice-topped fence partly seen at far right. Overlooked by the veranda but out of view, a Japanese-inspired garden, with boulders and plantings arranged around a lily pond and waterfall, is sheltered beneath a large oak to the far right.

Figure 125.

REAR "OUTDOOR ROOM" OF THE LOS ALTOS HOUSE.

Overlooked by the veranda, this inviting area's U-shaped enclosure is paved with a mix of flagstone and concrete. To fully exploit the relatively shallow depth of the rear yard (reduced by the new addition), the back of the fireplace is set close to the fence that parallels the rear service alley. An illusion of greater space is created by plantings that obscure the fence. Although it enjoys the self-contained feeling of a separate "room," this area also preserves a sense of openness to the rest of the garden. Airy pergola-type structures, which occur on three sides, have Craftsman-style lanterns that provide soft lighting at night. The wooden detailing, tapering piers and masonry treatment seen here recalls those of the front entry pergola (see Figure 120). Lower bench-height forms on either end also recall those dividing the front garden areas (see Figure 122). Plentiful concrete counter space includes a built-in gas-fired barbeque at right. Matching concrete is employed for the fireplace mantel and pair of built-in benches on either side.

Figure 126 (opposite).

FRONT DOOR OF THE LOS ALTOS HOUSE.

Before the remodel, the front door was a plain, oak-veneered slab with no cutouts for any glass. While likely original, it added little character, but its opening was retained for its generous width. Although the owners wanted to add art glass and sidelights, the entry hall's wall space allowed for only one sidelight on the right. While the home's façade is asymmetrical, the front door was deliberately centered on the porch's front gable and steps (seen in Figure 121). In order to achieve a convincing balance under those circumstances, a "blind sidelight" (of solid wood) was added to the left side of the door, which duplicates the size and form of the "real" sidelight. In the upper panel on the left, the new design includes a single wall sconce. From inside the entry hall, the asymmetrical design with a single sidelight feels well suited to that space. Handcrafted of solid mahogany, the newly-expanded door ensemble appears appropriate in scale and quality for this house. A popular period motif of wisteria (also growing on the porch) was chosen for the art glass. For subtle unity, the narrow linear elements applied to the wooden panels are also carried over into the art-glass design.

Figure 127 (above).

VERANDA OF THE LOS ALTOS HOUSE.

Viewed from the far end that overlaps the original part of the house, this looks toward the side garden at left, and to the back (seen in Figure 124 and 125). A dining area is in the foreground, and the far corner is furnished with comfortable wicker furniture. On the right, a pair of wall sconces indicates the location of french doors opening from the family room. Directly opposite these is a wide set of stairs that leads to the side garden. Overlooked by the veranda, a Japanese-inspired garden and pond are placed near a large oak tree (partly obscured by the posts), and some of the boulders around the pond are visible on the far left. Elements of the original front porch repeat here in the painted beadboard ceiling, the scale and detailing of the supporting posts, and masonry treatment. Division of the veranda ceiling by box beams was prompted by the linear proportions of the space. The beams help bring definition to the various areas of the veranda, and structural features guided their placement. The beams also defined the various locations for an array of Craftsman-style lanterns, that provide a festive glow in the evenings.

Figure 128 (opposite).

LIVING ROOM IN THE LOS ALTOS HOUSE.

Viewed from the entry hall, the living room space expands into an adjoining "parlor" through a broad open doorway, at right, which was the home's original dining room. From there, a pair of french doors and side windows opens onto the new veranda (see Figure 124 and 127). Reconditioned and refinished, original Douglas fir wainscoting and plate rails have survived in both areas. This room had box beams, but they were rebuilt to conceal new structural framing. Original cabinets with leaded-glass doors flank the fireplace, but the subtle art-glass accents in the windows above were added. The wood mantel and corbels replicate the originals. Before the remodel, the fireplace was faced in plain red brick, which dated to its previous reconstruction. The owners commissioned a new tile facing and hearth that adapts a period design by Greene & Greene. On a field of handmade tiles with a muted matte-green glaze, a meandering stylized vine and flower motif was plotted out. Using tiny ceramic chips and small square tiles in softly contrasting colors, that design was then meticulously inlaid. The handcrafted surround of brushed steel also adapts a Greene & Greene design. Furnishings combine Craftsman-style replicas with some period pieces.

Figure 129.

DINING ROOM IN THE LOS ALTOS HOUSE.

Newly crafted mahogany woodwork here contrasts with adjoining rooms, and includes a box-beam ceiling, built-in cabinets, wainscoting, and beveled-glass pocket doors. Abstracted floral motifs of the leaded art glass were inspired by period designs of Greene & Greene, and applied to a central lantern, wall sconces, and china cabinet doors. While part of the original house, this room never had such refined features, for it was the home's first kitchen. The present kitchen is in the new addition to the right, and part of the family room's stone fireplace is glimpsed (see Figure 130) through its door. A single french door at far right leads to the open terrace and side garden (seen in Figure 123). The entry hall is toward the left. The doorway to the parlor adjoining the living room was widened, and a handcrafted cabinet and center table commissioned for that room is partly visible. Beyond, another wide doorway connects to the family room. The far window is one of two that flank doors to the new veranda (also seen Figure 128). With a plain coved ceiling, the parlor was once the dining room, but that function was already assigned to this space long before the recent remodel.

Figure 130 (opposite).

FAMILY ROOM IN THE LOS ALTOS HOUSE.

Several signature elements of Craftsman-style interiors occur in the new family room. Period-style lanterns hang from intersecting box beams, and a colonnade separates the kitchen but maintains an open feeling. It is comprised of a pair of square, tapering columns set on lower cabinets facing the kitchen. Above, a deep beam that contains high, narrow cabinets facing the kitchen is fitted with backlit, leaded art-glass panels that feature stylized poppies. Similar panels adapting the ginkgo motif face toward the kitchen. The stone fireplace is placed on an axis with a wide doorway to the parlor (out of view at right) and can be seen from the living room. Above its thick mantel, a set of folding doors conceals a flat-screen television. Each door panel has a hand-carved poppy motif, and the delicate low-relief forms are highlighted with iridescent colored pigment. Below the windows, built-in cushioned benches look across the veranda toward the outdoor room (see Figure 125) in back. Out of view to the left, french doors open to the veranda (see Figure 127). In the kitchen's far corner, stairs to the art studio and a bathroom over the garage are partly visible through a doorway.

Figure 131 (right).

DETAIL OF SKYLIGHT IN THE LOS ALTOS HOUSE.

To bring more light to the second-floor hallway, a new skylight of trapezoidal form was framed by box beams and recessed into the ceiling. Seen at lower left is one of the area's handblown glass pendant fixtures. Initially, this was intended to admit daylight, but structural framing in the attic determined an artificial light source to be the most practical solution. A white-painted wooden box was constructed to house a series of fluorescent lights behind. Bulbs can be conveniently changed from the attic level via a pull-down stairs in the nearby master bedroom closet area. Inspired by oak trees shading the house, the stylized leaded art-glass design of delicate branches helps filter the light source. The effect closely approximates natural daylight.

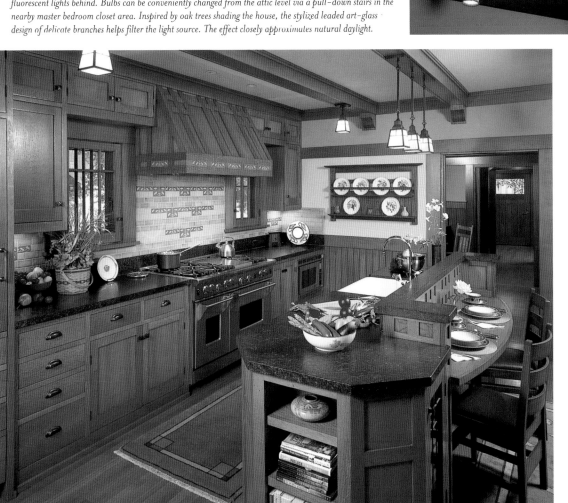

Figure 132.

KITCHEN IN THE LOS ALTOS HOUSE.

Prior to the remodel, the previous kitchen was in this same location. Reconstructed as part of the new addition, the kitchen is open to the family room (see Figure 130), and quartersawn oak woodwork is consistent in these areas. Recessed panel doors and flush-front drawers were modeled on period kitchen cabinetry. At far left, oak panels conceal a refrigerator and freezer drawer units. Dark greenish granite counters have a speckled texture and honed (matte) finish. Above the range and on the backsplash are alternating bands of handmade field tile. Low-relief accent tiles with a ginkgo leaf design combine their colors. These are also inset as a border on the range hood, where wood detailing near the top recalls the design above a curving dining-height oak surface on the island at right. Clipped corners and varying heights help reduce the island's mass. Craftsman-style pendant lighting hangs from box beams set on rounded corbels. Windows overlook the open terrace and side garden seen in Figure 123. Through the doorway and across the dining room to the left is a vestibule with service stairs that connect to both the second-floor and basement areas, as well as a door to the side garden. The basement was also remodeled into additional living space, and includes a new bathroom. The front door's art glass is glowing in the entry hall beyond.

Figure 133.

GUEST BATHROOM IN THE LOS ALTOS HOUSE.

No original bathrooms had survived, but this one's design is more closely based on period examples than the others. In the original part of the house, it is near the guest bedroom (see Figure 134) and directly above the dining room, with windows overlooking the side garden (seen in Figure 123). Simple linen curtains are stenciled with a period motif. Outlined in black, the glossy white subway tile wainscot is capped by a banding of Carrara marble bordered in black. The marble is repeated at the floor's perimeter and in the small octagonal tiles of the patterned inset, which is outlined and dotted in black. A cast-iron bathtub (out of view) is set into a decking of matching marble at left, with low cabinet doors on the side for plumbing access. A separate stall shower adjoins the tub in the near left corner, and on the opposite side is a door to the toilet enclosure. The curving lines and substantial front legs of the white porcelain sink replicate a period design. At far right is a built-in linen cabinet with drawers. Period-style plumbing hardware, fittings, and lighting are all nickel-plated. A blue-gray color enlivens the walls and also harmonizes with the tones of the marble.

Figure 134.

GUEST BEDROOM IN THE LOS ALTOS HOUSE.

In the original portion of the house, this former master bedroom is directly above the living room. Windows at left are in a front-facing gable (seen in Figures 120 and 121). This room was enlarged toward the right, borrowing its added space from a closet that once enclosed the smaller window at far right. Now open to the room, its original sash was fitted with art glass matching the nearby hallway skylight (see Figure 131). Centered on the fireplace, the wall's expanded proportions were manipulated using three new arching alcoves. To create their depth, the wall was furred out as needed, allowing for a built-in cushioned seat under an existing window at left. The window seat required more depth than the new gas insert for the fireplace, which was centered between the windows. Framing the fireplace are shallow, built-in display cabinets with leaded glass doors fitted with glass shelves and concealed lighting. Recessed to be flush with the wall's face, the cabinets have sconces above each, and small pendant lights occur in the alcoves to either side. The smaller window's sill height determined that of the built-in dresser below it, which in turn guided the height of the recessed mantel and adjoining cabinets. The fireplace and hearth tile's soft color palette, mottled matte finish, and low-relief figural accents reproduce period Batchelder designs. The wallpaper adapts a vintage William Morris pattern.

Figure 135 (opposite).

MASTER BEDROOM IN THE LOS ALTOS HOUSE.

Part of the new addition, this room is entered through double doors (partly glimpsed at far right) at the end of the second-floor hallway. A two-tiered, period-style fixture hangs from the vaulted peak of a beamed ceiling that was initially planned as flat. Only after the roof's rough framing went up did the owners opt to keep it open. The floors and all woodwork are Douglas fir. The ceiling's massive, squared beams were designed separately from the actual structural framing members, which are completely hidden. Beadboard sheathing is in between them. An exterior detail inspired the brackets (knee braces) below the beams, which link to the walls by moldings in a half-timbered effect. Single-story room proportions are implied by a horizontal frieze above the lower walls. Between a pair of narrow built-in cabinets, the fireplace has a bordered tile surround with low-relief panels and corbels that each replicate period Batchelder designs. Above it, paneled areas contain wall sconces and an inset beveled mirror. On the far wall opposite the bed, french doors with oversized sidelights open from the sitting area to a balcony (visible in Figure 123) with a private view over the side garden. Out of view at left is a trio of high horizontal windows (seen in Figure 124) in the upper rear gable.

Figure 136.

HOUSE IN BERKELEY, CALIFORNIA (1913; WITH RECENT ADDITIONS).

Framed by towering trees, this Northbrae area home is a blending of the Shingle and Craftsman styles. There is also English influence in the massing of its sweeping gabled roofline. Designed by local architect Charles Sumner Kaiser, the house commands distant views from the rear that extend across the bay to the Golden Gate Bridge. These were among the guiding factors in planning the addition of a new garage and studio structure that was recently built on the downhill slope behind the house (partly glimpsed at right). At the same time, a new front landscaping scheme was replanted in this area with an informal, natural look. Significant hardscape elements were also added, including new brick paving for the driveway that connects to the recessed front porch. Nearby, a Craftsman-style lantern sits on a low, square brick post of vintage, salvaged clinker brick. This matches a pair of monumental square columns, mounted with similar larger lanterns, that support a set of hand-wrought iron driveway gates at right. Inset in front with handmade tile panels, the large columns are hollow, with access doors on their opposite sides to allow for inside storage. Substantial wood and concrete benches replicate a period design originally created for a local public park by important Bay Area architect Julia Morgan.

Figure 137 (opposite).

REAR ROOF DECK BRIDGE OF THE BERKELEY HOUSE.

While its historic street-side demeanor was maintained, the home's rear additions interpret a decidedly contemporary approach, yet the new work was conceived with respect for the existing structure. Little of the new construction actually abuts the original house, so it more easily coexists with the new design elements. To preserve views from the main living level, the addition could not exceed the height of the home's walkout basement, so both the living and dining rooms now overlook a deck created on the roof of the added garage and studio. By way of a bridge toward the right, the link to the house was made through an existing pergola-covered balcony (partially enclosed by glass) that adjoins the main public rooms. Attached to the bridge, a compact spiral stairs allows for convenient outside circulation to the other outdoor living areas below. Prompted by a mature wisteria already trained up the back of the house, the design of the new railings utilizes open stainless-steel grids to support extensions of the fast-growing vine. This softening effect on the new structure will also greatly expand the display of future wisteria blooms, and help to further blend it with the lines of the original house.

Figure 138 (right).

REAR TERRACE DETAIL
OF THE BERKELEY HOUSE.

From the pool area seen in Figure 139, the tile-accented concrete paving continues into this open terrace. Above the new studio and garage, part of the roof deck has a glass-paneled railing to pre-serve the view. A stucco-faced outdoor pizza oven has an octago-nal hooded form rising into a similarly angled chimney that is inset with period ceramic tile. Above wood storage space, a raised tiled hearth wraps around the arched oven opening, and adjoins a matching countertop over a compact refrigerator and sink unit. A wall-mounted Craftsman-style lantern lights this area at night. To the left of the oven, a wide doorway opens to the studio portion of the garage. It is fitted with a sliding "barn door" suspended from a concealed track, which cantilevers as shown off the back of the building when opened. Due to the sloping lot, this terrace remains above ground by a full story; to the left of the door, a stairway leads to the lower garden. A solid low railing wall inset with more tile incorporates a built-in bench partly seen at left.

Figure 139 (below).

LOWER REAR AREA
OF THE BERKELEY HOUSE.

Viewed from the lower level, the supporting understructure of the bridge is entirely finished in natural wood. Its revealed construction makes an abstracted reference to the home's Arts and Crafts sensibility. Substantial square columns and crossbeams extend from beneath the bridge to span a compact above ground pool, at right, with a built-in current. An out-side door to the basement level is directly underneath the bridge. Out of view to the right, a gate opens to a side walkway connecting uphill to an outside kitchen door and the street. To the left of the spiral stairs, blooming wisteria hovers over a gate that leads to the driveway turn-around in front of the garage (out of view to the left). Paving includes some slate tiles on a ramp made for a slight level change at left, but is mostly concrete scored into diagonal squares. Best seen in Figure 138, each intersection of these squares is inset with an early-twentieth-cen-tury ceramic tile, which makes an effective place to display some of the owners' extensive collection. With another vintage low-relief tile inset nearby, a fanciful cast-stone face gazes out from the pool's outside corner.

Figure 140.

HOUSE IN SAN DIEGO, CALIFORNIA (C1910; WITH RECENT ADDITIONS).

From the street, this home in the Mission Hills area makes a convincing impression as an intact period design, but it was first built as a typical single-story Craftsman-style bungalow. Its recent expansion has yielded a new open kitchen and family room area added to the back, as well as a master bedroom, bathroom, and study in a partial second-story addition. Off a rear service alley, a detached garage was entirely rebuilt and now includes a second-floor art studio. The project faced the common limitations of a narrow urban lot but also had minimal rear expansion space. Its low-pitched gabled roof enclosed an attic that was useful only for storage, so further upward expansion was pursued. Extending only above the rear half of the existing home, the addition is minimally intrusive and well proportioned. Limiting the new design's forms and detailing to adaptations of existing originals helped ensure its cohesion. Now a three-gabled, shingled composition, the home has a new upper gable that transforms the façade. Its projecting center section, resulting in a pair of jogs in the eaves, helps relieve the new gable's mass. Adapted original elements on the addition include the projecting roof beams (purlins), "half-timbering" with a V-shaped molding profile, pointy window casings, and linear sash design. In the foreground, a low retaining wall of river rock with a concrete cap adjoins a pair of low matching piers, mounted with lanterns, that frame the front entry walk. A diagonally-angled front door as seen here is more typical of homes with corner sites.

Figure 141 (opposite).

KITCHEN AREA IN THE SAN DIEGO HOUSE.

A practical, plausible flow between old and new interior spaces preserved the original living and dining room toward the front of the house. Circulation between the front and rear areas occurs through either a kitchen doorway to the dining room (their spatial relationship was unchanged) or a hallway (out of view, on the left) that once connected to a rear bedroom (absorbed by the remodel). Interpreting period style with contemporary features, the new kitchen employs simply detailed, white-painted cabinets, a compact island with a second sink, utilitarian period-style lighting, and thick-profile granite countertops. Seen from the family room area (in Figure 142), the kitchen is framed by a pair of square, tapering columns set on high piers that adapt a period-style colonnade. A familiar Craftsman-style form, this example is interpreted with more vertical proportions than most. A response to the addition's higher ceilings, it also helps ensure the area's spacious feeling. An open counter at left expands dining or serving options. At right, a classic breakfast nook was created, which has a built-in table with bench seating over deep pull-out drawers.

Figure 144 (left).

MASTER BEDROOM IN THE SAN DIEGO HOUSE.

This retreat on the new partial second floor feels far removed from the other areas. Its lower ceiling height and crossing box beams with attached lighting re-create the proportion of a typical Craftsman interior. White-painted woodwork is offset by the natural wood used around the fireplace. Squared pilasters with shallow recessed panels are aligned with the box beams above, and also frame the expansive tile surround of the fireplace and hearth. The recessed insert's raised height allows for greater visibility from the bed. Muted colors and matte-finished mottled glazes in the handmade ceramic field tiles, borders, and low-relief accents re-create an Arts and Crafts sensibility. In lieu of any mantel, the upper center of the tilework has an inset panel with a wooded landscape motif. At left, two (of three) windows in the front-facing gable are visible (seen in Figure 140); the other is in the adjoining master bathroom. An attic storage space access panel is visible under the larger window.

Figure 142 (opposite).

FAMILY ROOM AREA IN THE SAN DIEGO HOUSE.

Open to the kitchen (seen in Figure 141), the new family room also provides circulation space to the new garage, garden, and second-floor areas. Additional square footage was gained by squaring off the original rear wall's irregular outline and by extending it back a few feet. Detailed to match the house, the reconstructed rear garage is partly visible behind. French doors open to a covered area under an open bridge (partly seen in Figure 143). A bright and roomy staircase was placed into the right corner. The oversized, square, tapering newel posts framing the lower landing amplify its presence. The posts resemble similarly shaped columns across the room, seen in Figure 141. Built-in lanterns are inset with softly colored slag glass. The posts' staggered forms and ribbed piers have a sleek sculptural quality. Consistent throughout both old and new areas is the use of casement (swinging) windows with a crossing linear sash design typical of the Craftsman style.

Figure 143 (right).

STAIR HALL IN THE SAN DIEGO HOUSE.

The vertical proportions of this brightly lit space are complemented by simple, consistently linear motifs expressed in each of its primary design elements. A triple-light ceiling fixture echoes the three-part stairwell window on the left, whose tall narrow panels align at the top but are stepped in height below, to reflect the angled rise of the stairs. The two newel posts occurring at the stair turns repeat the lantern-topped design of those seen in the family room (see Figure 141), while the third one's form suggests a smaller-scale sibling. Their rich wood finish contrasts with painted, square-spindled railings. Partly seen through a french door at left, an open wooden bridge makes a direct connection between this level and the second floor of the new garage, which contains a frequently used art studio. This convenient feature saves steps and time for the owners, and also conserves open space in the small yard below. Out of view to the left, a door leads to a study in the addition's other rear corner. Opposite the french door is a short hall leading to the master bedroom.

Figure 145 (below).

MASTER BATHROOM FIREPLACE AND TUB IN THE SAN DIEGO HOUSE.

With a winking nod to Arts and Crafts design traditions, the new master bathroom departs from the greater restraint seen in the adjoining bedroom (Figure 143). What was not apparent in that view is that the fireplace insert is two-sided, and also faces into the bathroom. Above the tub, this fireplace tile surround is simpler in its form and coloring, and has just two small low-relief accents. An unusual raised hearth is topped by a marble slab of related color. It conforms to the tub's curving sides to create a form-fitting niche, which is faced in matching tile and terminates into stepped ends on either side. Used to display art pottery, a boldly scaled mantel is comprised of massive (but shallow) squared shelves. It has stepped corbels that recall the shape of the hearth's tiled-end detailing. Period pedestal tubs inspired the form of this new oval example.

Figure 146 (above).

MASTER BATHROOM DETAIL IN THE SAN DIEGO HOUSE.

The master bathroom's design shows other nods to period tradition, such as the small hexagonal tiles of white porcelain for flooring (with occasional black accents). In the far left corner, the walls of a roomy, glass-enclosed walk-in shower are lined floor-to-ceiling with white glazed subway tiles. The showerhead is mounted from the ceiling; nickel-plated fixtures are seen throughout. Marble matching the tub area is used on the shower's built-in bench and for its tile-sided threshold. Characterized by two of everything, the egalitarian design of the area to the right boasts a separate toilet compartment on either side (the door of one is seen at center). A beam trimmed with crown molding and a pair of corbels is supported by a tapering wooden column, which is attached to the cabinets of a pair of mirror-image vanities. Countertop areas repeat the room's marble and tile. With a free-floating effect, a large wood-framed mirror sits on a raised base between sinks and is attached to the ceiling. Sconces are mounted on each opposing side of its glass.

Figure 147.

ORCHARD HOUSE, COLORADO (1917–1936).

Set against the Rocky Mountain foothills, this home was designed and built by William Herzer for his own residence. In an Arts and Crafts scenario, he gathered rocks from the open hillside behind the house and built it by himself. While working full-time as a postman, he did all the design and building in his spare time, but it took many years. The house was mostly built in the 1920s, but site construction extended into the mid-1930s, to complete outbuildings for an apple-farming enterprise he had established. Some of his original trees survive in the remains of the orchard, and the current owners named their home to honor Herzer's efforts. Conceived in the eclectic style mode of historic revivalism, there is English influence in the home's steeply pitched, dormered, and gabled roof forms. Asymmetrically composed, its angled mass pivots around a tower form with a pointed roof cap. The walls' irregular stonework accents various arched openings. The angled wing at right contains the kitchen and dining area, and a pergola-topped terrace adjoining the living room extends to the left. This was designed to be the front, but a recent major remodel shifted the main entrance to the other side, so now it functions as the garden façade.

Figure 148.

ENTRY FAÇADE OF ORCHARD HOUSE.

In the distance at right, the plains' horizon line stretches eastward from the foothills. Wintry weather was a consideration in relocating the front entrance from the opposite side, and the new uphill entry has proven a useful year-round convenience for the owners and visitors alike. Under a pergola-topped terrace, partly seen at right (and in Figure 147), an enclosed garage has direct access into the basement level of the house. Passing close to the front door, a curving driveway is sheltered beneath an oversized, steeply gabled porte-cochère *added during the remodel. With distinctively crossing, exposed trusswork in an open gable, its sharply angled form echoes the dormers behind it. Such steep roofs also readily shed snow. Built of matching local stone, massive tapering columns in the Craftsman style support the open end. Showing the home's shallow depth, daylight through the front door is passing through the aligned former entry door (in Figure 147), and on the left is part of the angled wing. Out of view at left is a new and similarly-styled guesthouse by the old orchard (see Figure 156).*

Figure 149 (right).

FRONT ENTRY DETAIL OF ORCHARD HOUSE.

Creating a rhythmic lineup of exposed structure, the same kind of trusswork in the porte-cochère's *open gable end (seen in Figure 148) repeats at intervals along its length. Combined with the roof's sharp pitch, the pencil-pointed vertical elements of each truss have a Gothic-inspired effect recalling forms of early English Arts and Crafts architecture. The decorative iron strap hinges on the wood-planked front door and peaked wall sconces also imply a similar influence, which is also interpreted in various interior areas (see Figures 150–55). In contrast to the plain asphalt, irregularly sized flagstone paving in this area gives it a sense of refinement. What might have been perceived as merely part of the driveway becomes a transitional outdoor "anteroom" for the interior. The roof structure is supported by a pair of stone pilasters attached to the face of the building, which correspond in form and scale to the freestanding columns at the opposite end (seen in Figure 148).*

Figure 150 (above).

DINING AND KITCHEN AREA IN ORCHARD HOUSE.

A pair of sconces that re-create a Gustav Stickley design flank a deep doorway from the entry hall (partly seen in Figure 153) to the shared dining and kitchen areas in the angled wing. Out of view are two tall, arch-topped windows in the dining area (seen in Figure 147) that face the rear garden. While combining both of these room functions sets an informal tone, the dining area is enriched by fine period antiques. Discreetly placed lighting sources create a variety of effects at night. A vintage, bowl-shaped art-glass shade defines the dining area. A long, narrow trestle table maximizes the area's available space, and exploits the room's width to its advantage. A set of nineteenth-century English Gothic Revival dining chairs continues an influence that extends throughout the home. An island at the center of the U-shaped kitchen (obscured by the floral arrangement) allows for convenient serving near the table. Dominated by its finely crafted wood cabinetry, the kitchen was designed to form an elegant backdrop. In the dark gray stone of the backsplash and countertops, scatterings of various embedded fossil forms contribute interest and a subtle texture.

Figure 151 (above).

LIVING ROOM IN ORCHARD HOUSE.

In contrast to the entry hall (seen through the doorway at right), the living room has a more intimate scale. Its peachy-yellow walls and outlooks on three sides create an inviting atmosphere. Opposite the doorway, french doors to a pergola-topped open terrace (seen in Figures 147 and 148) also adjoin the rear garden area. The windows at left face towards the front driveway. Refined Craftsman character is contributed by new crown moldings, ceiling beams, as well as door and window casings. To conserve floor space, the new fireplace's depth was mostly absorbed into the wall thickness. Traditional English-inspired forms are interpreted in the mantel design. Its arching form frames a stepped tile surround and hearth of period-style Batchelder designs. A moody painting above, called "Meditation" (c1915), is by progressive Austrian painter Sergei Pahnre. The wall sconces are handcrafted replicas of Gustav Stickley designs. Period furnishings are an eclectic blending of styles and periods. Probably a mid-nineteenth-century American synagogue altar seat, the hand-carved armchair at right features unusual motifs of camels' heads and feet.

Figure 152 (left).

STAIRCASE IN ORCHARD HOUSE.

Next to the front door (out of view to the left), the staircase is the interior's most defining feature. Meticulously handcrafted, it is comprised of a series of slender, pointed newel posts, and cutout railing boards (also seen in Figure 153) with a vertical emphasis. It recalls Gothic designs that inspired the early English Arts and Crafts movement. The entry hall's paneled walls extend into a board-and-batten wainscot continuing up the stairs. In the stairwell, a leaded art-glass window—its fruit-laden bough motif references the history of Orchard House—is set into a diminutive dormer window (seen in Figure 147). At the foot of the stairs, period pieces include a bench by Gustav Stickley and a Tiffany art-glass floor lamp. The basement level is reached by stairs through the doorway to the right, where recently developed informal living spaces have direct access to the garage. Specific inspiration for this staircase came from the one in "Red House" (named for its brick color), the 1859 home of William Morris, the early leading proponent of the English Arts and Crafts movement. Coincidentally, Morris sited that home in an old orchard.

Figure 153.

ENTRY HALL AND LIBRARY AREA IN ORCHARD HOUSE.

Inside the front door, the entry hall's asymmetrical form helps to arrange its space into separate zones. Seen at left is part of the new staircase's slender pointed newel post and peaked cutout railing boards, which establish an English Arts and Crafts influence. The post's form recalls (in reversed direction) a similar Gothic-inspired detail in the porte-cochère's *open trusswork (seen in Figure 149). With unexpected natural specimens displayed among the volumes, full-height bookcases continue past the living room doorway on the right into a library area at the far end. The clipped upper corners of the french door (where the front door was originally) echo that area's faceted outline. In lieu of any nearby window, the door admits daylight and garden views to the space. An antique tall-case clock stands to one side of a wider opening into the dining area and kitchen, which is partly visible beyond (see Figure 150). Wooden beams, with unusual slotted detailing along their undersides, are set off by a gold-colored painted ceiling finish, softly blended into the green-shaded edges of the frieze.*

Figure 154.

MASTER BEDROOM IN ORCHARD HOUSE.

The Gothic-derived influences of English Arts and Crafts design inspired the concept for the new master bedroom. Occupying one side of the second floor, its location can be seen in Figure 147 to the left of the tower, which contains the adjoining master bathroom. The irregular meeting of the wall and ceiling areas and the narrow dormer windows contribute to the room's appeal. Superbly crafted, full-height paneling is on the bed wall. The headboard has an applied Gothic-arch motif. A partial tester (canopy) supports side hangings made of a lined period textile. Another vintage textile is used for the bedspread. The footboard has a "blind arcade" of repeating Gothic arches and panels set between two bedposts with faceted octagonal finials. Arts and Crafts–period lamps sit on nineteenth-century nightstands. The insets of the paneling have chamfered (beveled) corners, a medieval furniture detail that reappeared in both Gothic Revival and later English Arts and Crafts designs. With a flattened Tudor arch above its doorway, the short hallway at right has two closets on the left and connects to the stair hall. The tower bathroom, opposite the closet doors, is out of view to the right.

Figure 155 (opposite).

MASTER BEDROOM DETAIL IN ORCHARD HOUSE.

Viewed over the bed's footboard are open built-in bookcases, where the display of an unexpected range of exotic collectibles among the books recalls the tradition of a "cabinet of curiosities" (a conceit of worldy collectors that was fashionable in grand seventeenth- and eighteenth-century European homes). A glossy, pearlescent green paint applied to the walls and ceiling reflects light. The dormer windows are detailed with arching top panels (one is at left). The window at right, in a large roof gable end, has an arched soffit that creates a shallow recessed alcove. It is fitted with sliding wood shutters, paneled and detailed like the wainscoting (seen at left), which are shown partly extended. Below is an early English Arts and Crafts library table (and similarly styled side chair), with cutouts and joinery details derived from actual Gothic furniture. Without superfluous ornament, these follow the Arts and Crafts tenet of revealed construction. A vintage "invalid chair" on wheels (with an extendible footrest) sits by a floor lamp with a Gothic motif on its mica shade. A walk-in closet is out of view to the right.

Figure 156 (above).

POOL AND SPA AREA OF ORCHARD HOUSE.

This view shows the stand of mature trees that were blended with outdoor amenities recently added near the main house (out of view, toward the left). Rising up behind are the rock-strewn foothills from which William Herzer gathered his building materials. To contrast with his predominantly irregular stonework, a crisp rectangular form was chosen for the pool, and diagonally set, square flagstone paving surrounds it. The rocky outcropping seen at upper right is reflected in the deep blue-green water. A bubbling circular spa has a retractable cover that vanishes into a low stone enclosure to the left. Recalling a natural rock formation, a massive outdoor fireplace with a broad stone hearth anchors a dining area at the far right. It abuts the end of a new guesthouse, whose foundation level was built by Herzer as an apple cellar to adjoin his orchard (downhill on the right side). Partly seen at left is another stone outbuilding he constructed as a small summerhouse. With battered (sloping) walls that seem to have grown out of the boulders at its base, it adjoins the right side of the garden area that extends from the home's former front façade (seen in Figure 147).

Recent Arrivals
Brand New Homes of the Arts & Crafts Revival

The Lure of the New

Not every fan of vintage Arts and Crafts homes is up to the task of taking on the rigors of an old-house makeover. Many of those who have done so will attest it is a process that simply never seems to end. Fortunately for those who love the design sensibility of this historic period but opt for a new-house interpretation of it, there are now more alternatives than ever to consider. The following examples show a broad range of approaches in expressing an Arts and Crafts influence in the design of newly constructed homes.

A pent-up demand for new housing stock that reflects Arts and Crafts sensibilities has triggered a growing trend. In the early years of the movement's revival, the architecture and design community initially responded with a flurry of essentially contemporary, light-filled residential designs that made timid gestures to incorporate some semblance of Arts and Crafts–derived detailing. Usually the attempts to interpret this influence was most apparent on the homes' exteriors. Sometimes such endeavors were admired as quite artistically successful, while others came off as pandering, or superficial, in comparison to most period examples. Some of these designs sported only a few token Craftsman-style elements that were simply grafted onto an otherwise entirely contemporary house. Especially if they were already collectors of the period's antiques, prospective homeowners who wanted to build a new house in the Craftsman style at that time were often surprised to find they knew more about the Arts and Crafts movement (and its related architecture) than some of the design professionals they interviewed. Fortunately, this is a less common occurrence today.

A Brightening Picture

Although still evolving, the phenomenon of new Arts and Crafts–inspired homes has produced increasingly sophisticated designs in recent years. This is partly because many design professionals are better educated now about the style, and therefore more likely to be adept and experienced at interpreting it. Also this is partly a result of greater public awareness and respect for historic architecture in general, largely achieved through the efforts and success of the preservation movement. Additional assistance has come from an ever-growing wealth of resource material in the form of specialized books, periodicals, products, and services for and about Arts and Crafts houses (both old and new). All of these factors have helped advance the caliber of new period-revival homes. Some new homes can now be compared quite favorably with, and some would argue might surpass, their celebrated predecessors. Although certainly a good sign, such subjective observations have little bearing on this particular discussion.

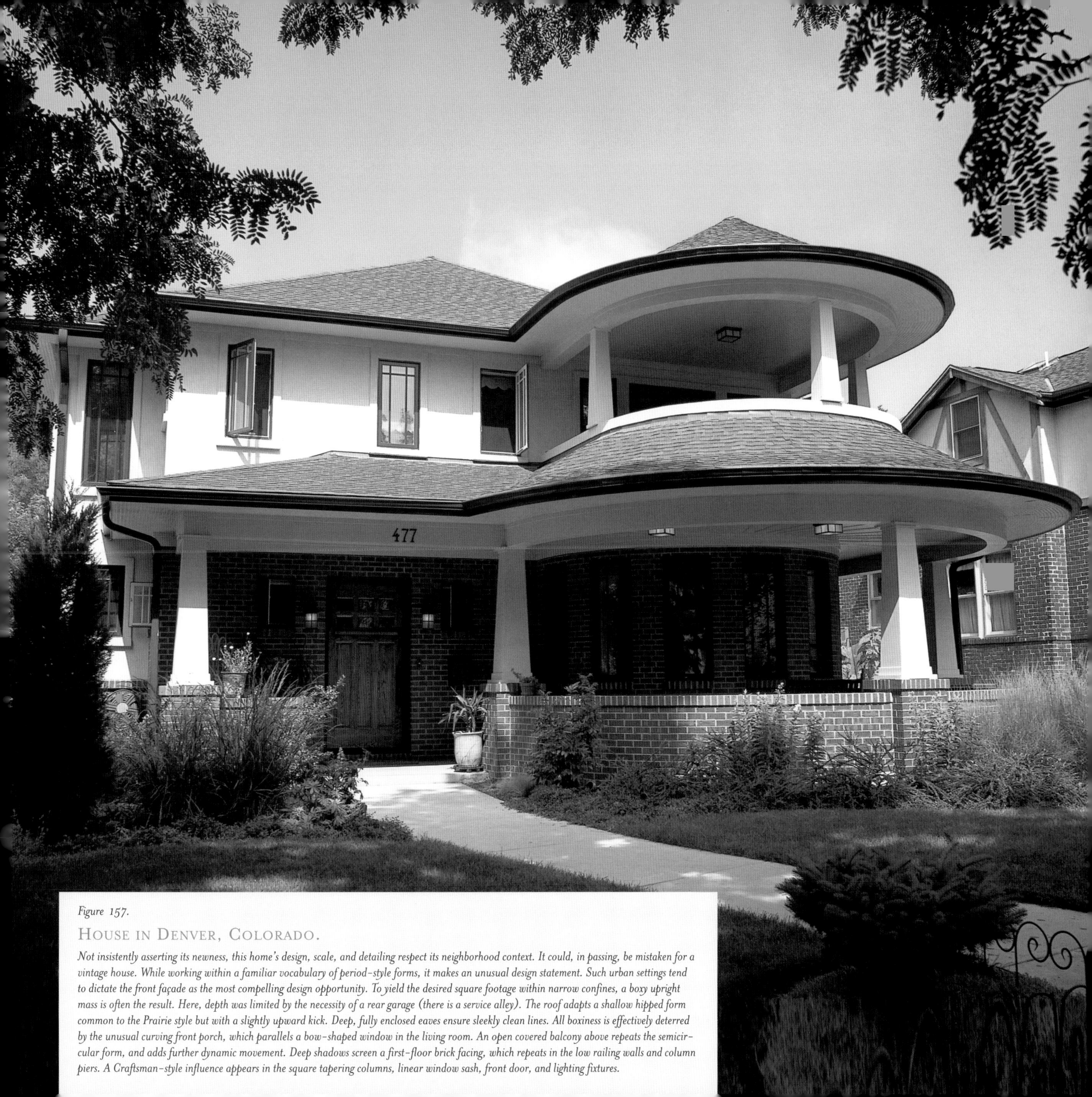

Figure 157.

HOUSE IN DENVER, COLORADO.

Not insistently asserting its newness, this home's design, scale, and detailing respect its neighborhood context. It could, in passing, be mistaken for a vintage house. While working within a familiar vocabulary of period-style forms, it makes an unusual design statement. Such urban settings tend to dictate the front façade as the most compelling design opportunity. To yield the desired square footage within narrow confines, a boxy upright mass is often the result. Here, depth was limited by the necessity of a rear garage (there is a service alley). The roof adapts a shallow hipped form common to the Prairie style but with a slightly upward kick. Deep, fully enclosed eaves ensure sleekly clean lines. All boxiness is effectively deterred by the unusual curving front porch, which parallels a bow-shaped window in the living room. An open covered balcony above repeats the semicircular form, and adds further dynamic movement. Deep shadows screen a first-floor brick facing, which repeats in the low railing walls and column piers. A Craftsman-style influence appears in the square tapering columns, linear window sash, front door, and lighting fixtures.

It is interesting to note that many prospective new-house clients most likely to respond to the Arts and Crafts aesthetic were once avid Modernists. Some had been first drawn to the spare elegance of Modernism, yet disdained its potential lack of warmth. Other "ex-Modernists" took tenuous detours into the Victorian world for a time, but are now finding themselves ready to retreat back to greater simplicity. For many a lapsed Modernist, it is quite a revelation to finally realize that, all along, the simple comfort and homey warmth they always sought can be found in Arts and Crafts–inspired design. And, like Modernism, it also comes with the trappings of its own design philosophy to ponder. In fact, this particular aspect deepens the enjoyment and appreciation of Arts and Crafts design and architecture significantly for many of its adherents, likely to a far greater extent today than was the case during the original movement's fairly brief duration in America.

An Enduring Choice

Historically, Americans have responded with great enthusiasm to newness. Part of the appeal of building a new home is the satisfaction derived from having the freedom to create (budget permitting) whatever one desires. With this powerful appeal, the new house phenomenon is an enduring one in whatever style may be selected.

This chapter makes its case with some very creative, new Arts and Crafts–inspired interpretations. Moreover, what is apparent in all of the following homes is that they are unabashedly new, and not illusory stage sets that strive to precisely recreate the past.

While some of the following examples had building budgets more generous than most, each is brimming with design concepts and details that could potentially be reinterpreted under more modest circumstances. They could certainly also inform some old-house remodels as well. These examples were chosen to appear here because they are, in large part, idea houses. While the Craftsman style tends to dominate the playing field, some of these homes utilize the same crossover influences (e.g., the Shingle, Prairie, Colonial Revival styles) that "cross-pollinated" many of the vintage examples seen in previous chapters. Others are more emphatically contemporary in their approach and feeling, and pointedly demonstrate that Arts and Crafts influence can be very broadly interpreted. In reviewing these homes, it is fascinating to speculate just how they might be perceived in another century or two, or three. Like some of their surviving predecessors, let us hope that they, too, will still be around to inform, charm, and perhaps amaze the old-house fans of the future.

Figure 158.

HOUSE IN CAMBRIA, CALIFORNIA.

This two-story home skillfully expresses Craftsman taste, with robustly scaled rafter tails extending beyond its deep eaves. Surrounded by trees, it required a close-range view, and remains partly obscured. The front façade at left extends forward in a centrally placed gabled portion that creates a deep living room bay, and an upper balcony off the master bedroom. Horizontal boards and a planter box detail the balcony railing. Matching chimneys are integral to this projection's imposing form. Absorbed into its first-floor walls, they first emerge to form a recess for the balcony's french doors before rising above the roof. A series of large structural beams with stepped ends are visible over the balcony on the gabled roof eaves. The beams' stepped motif repeats in the ends of the fascia boards of the gable and in corbels supporting the window boxes. An outside door from the dining room, flanked by lanterns, has a curving Shingle-style overhang like an awning. Partly seen at right is a gabled, window-lined breakfast room with a semi-octagonal bay above it. Accents of river rock occur at the home's lower outside corners. Out of view on the far left side, a porte-cochère *spans the driveway, and also shelters the front door.*

Figure 159 (left).

HOUSE IN RICHMOND BEACH, WASHINGTON.

Set against towering fir trees, this home's uphill site has sweeping water views. Not apparent here, the house has an L-shaped plan, and extends toward the back on the right side. Primarily interpreting the Shingle style, this design evokes the inventive and progressive character pervading the best period examples, which were also favored for similarly informal waterside settings. The shingled walls, angular gambrel-roofed gables, and shallow eaves each recall the style. In context with classical columns on the front pergola, this gambrel roof also makes a Colonial Revival reference, for that style also utilized it; in the period, the two styles were often combined. Distinctive details here include a chimney that skewers the projecting left gable, a balcony notched into the roof (its solid railing vertically extends an angled living room bay), and a small V-shaped bay in the gable peak at right. With a "reverse plan," its main entry is on the back of the left side. This allows the outdoor area in front (with the best view) to function as a private living space adjoining the main public rooms, instead of being a typical front entry porch. Plantings help buffer the raised terrace from the street. Visitors are guided uphill by paving on the left side leading toward the main entry.

Figure 160.

APPROACH TO
A HOUSE IN LAFAYETTE, CALIFORNIA.

A steeply sloping downhill site presented challenges in the design of this home. A blending of Craftsman and Shingle-style influences, the final solution was practically and artfully resolved. Buildings on such steep sites generally require their garages to be nearly level with the street, and the visual impact of the house, often set behind or below it, is often eclipsed. Here, the garage is also at street level (at upper left) but its integration with the house by attachment and shared details establishes a seamless connection. At street level, the main entry gate (partly visible at right) is marked by a small-scale pergola feature, high-lighting the point of entry. The portion of the structure at left is linked to the entry gate by a gently curving shingled wall that extends in three stepped sections from its front corner, following the line of a driveway turnout. This gesture directs visitors toward the gate and also influences the gracefully turning path of the brick staircase as it descends through a hillside garden to the entry area.

Figure 161 (above).

COURTYARD AREA OF
THE LAFAYETTE HOUSE.

Connected by an arching "bridge" (also seen in Figure 162), this home has two sections that enclose a sheltered and surprisingly level private courtyard area. In the uphill portion at left, the garage is on the far side of its top level. The bridge allows for garage access without venturing outside from the home's primary living spaces (situated in the right-hand portion). On the left, a home office space and separate guest quarters are oriented toward the courtyard. That side includes a shallow, window-lined top floor bay resting on curving shingled brackets, which overhangs a balcony (or a "loggia," when enclosed on three sides) with a square-spindled railing. Directly below, an oversized arched opening, repeating the form of the bridge, frames a recessed inglenook open to the lawn area. Although a classic and coveted period feature indoors, an inglenook is an unexpected outdoor amenity. Set into a wall faced with river rock, its fireplace is appropriately flanked by built-in benches. Opening to a curving stone-paved terrace, french doors at right lead to a spacious open kitchen (toward the bridge) and family room area. Also on this level, the living and dining room are within the gabled portion adjoining the bridge. At right, second-floor bedroom walls flare outward at the bottom, a Shingle-style detail that sheds water away from the building. In all the gables, oversized Craftsman-style brackets (knee braces) support the eaves.

Figure 162 (opposite).

ENTRY DETAIL OF THE LAFAYETTE HOUSE.

A closer look within the arch of the bridge between the two portions of the house shows its painted beadboard ceiling. Craftsman style is reflected in the design of the various matching lanterns and in the front door at right, which has four divided lights above its tapering inset panels. The small window next to it is partly visible in Figure 163. A typical Shingle-style detail, three concentric shingle courses frame the arch in the foreground, providing subtle emphasis. The paving of randomly sized stones that continues into the adjoining terrace area (seen in Figure 161) is more apparent in this view. The steps seen through the arch are made to match those of the main flight of brick entry stairs to the street (seen in Figure 160), which are out of view toward the left.

Figure 163 (above).

ENTRY HALL AND DINING ROOM IN THE LAFAYETTE HOUSE.

The small window partly seen at far left is by the front door (see Figure 162). A wide entry hall is lit by period-inspired fixtures, and extends to the living room at its opposite end. The open kitchen and family room areas are to the left. A long carpet runner has a pattern of oversized, abstracted ginkgo leaves, a favorite period motif. Configured around a built-in L-shaped bench, the staircase rises through a curving ceiling cutout. The dining room at right is almost entirely open to the hallway. French doors with a transom on its outside wall admit light and views across the room into the hall. Crossing box beams suspend small pendant lights around a central matching Craftsman-style fixture. High wainscot paneling has a plate rail, and above is a framed accent band painted a deep red. The board-and-batten detailing is repeated in the hallway. A typical period-style, recessed built-in sideboard has a mirror-backed serving surface. The oak flooring throughout features inlaid pinstripe accents with period-style "knot" details at each corner. Furnishings adapt vintage Craftsman examples.

Figure 164 (opposite).

OUTDOOR LIVING ROOM OF A HOUSE IN DEL MAR, CALIFORNIA.

Entered through a substantially scaled, Japanese-inspired covered gateway (partly seen at right), this home is fronted by a lush, walled tropical garden that upon entry evokes a feeling of calm and closeness to nature. A raised water garden built against the stucco-faced front wall is seen from this area. The single-story home's consistently informal open planning, use of simple forms, and straightforward detailing reflects an abstracted Arts and Crafts sensibility interpreted with an Asian-inspired feeling. Epitomizing the concept of indoor-outdoor living, this room is sheltered beneath a wooden ceiling of exposed structural elements. Its outside corner at left is secured around a massively scaled, stacked-stone fireplace. Both its raised hearth and shallow mantel are of cast concrete. The angled fireplace allows unobstructed views of both fire and garden from any spot in the space. A row of tall glass doors also overlook it from the living room (out of view toward the far left). The partial-height wall at left is connected to the house. Flooring is of practical slate squares that add texture and subtle colors. A square, stuccoed column at far right also supports the roof, which shelters an adjacent area by the front door.

Figure 165.

POOL AND MASTER BEDROOM WING OF THE DEL MAR HOUSE.

From most angles, this house is largely obscured by vegetation, but a clearing for the pool area provides this perspective. The building is angled around the contour of a steep hillside, which drops off toward the right. Partly seen at right, the home's primary portion is comprised of a low rectangular form with a shallow-pitched, end-gabled roof. A raised deck off the living and dining areas has steps to a flagstone path connecting to the pool area. An attached garage is out of view on the far side. Separated by an interior level change and sheltered under its own low-slung hipped roof, the master bedroom wing was designed to resemble and feel like a separate structure. A tall, airy covered porch across its end lends it the languid look of a tropical bungalow. More irregular flagstone set into the lawn informally defines the patio area between the porch and a long, narrow rectangular pool. It is edged on three sides by square flagstone slabs. Rising from the water along the fourth side (partly seen at left) is a stacked-stone retaining wall capped with matching flagstone.

Figure 166 (right).

HOUSE IN SACRAMENTO, CALIFORNIA.

Built over several years, this meticulously hand-crafted riverside home is surrounded by mature oaks. Interpreting mostly the Craftsman and Shingle styles, the home's welcoming lodge-like character belies its considerable size. With a primarily hipped roof, the home also employs gables to express different portions, which break up its mass. Throughout, Craftsman detailing occurs in brackets (knee braces), rafter tails, corbels, and leaded art glass. Irregularly laid shingled walls and diamond patterned insets add strong texture. Hooded forms over smaller second-floor windows are a Shingle-style detail in the gabled portion at right. A secondary gable extends over the bay windows, whose form and detailing varies by level. Rising from rounded planters, arching brick panels relieve lower wall expanses of rough granite facing. The front façade is mostly symmetrical and is centered on the covered two-story entry porch. Fronted by a stone terrace, it is comprised of monumental pairs of square wood columns that rest on connected stone and brick piers. Lantern-mounted, the columns rise to terminate in bold groupings of arched crossing brackets that support the hipped roof. Visible within the porch, above the front door, are cutout railing boards on a recessed balcony. Next to the porch, a naturalistic waterfall feeds a meandering, boulder-lined stream and pond extending along the walkway to the right.

Figure 167 (left).

COVERED FRONT WALKWAY OF THE SACRAMENTO HOUSE.

Craftsman-style lanterns line a covered, slate-paved walkway that connects the garage area at right to the main house toward the left. The positioning of the garage creates an L-shaped configuration with the house. At the far end, the arched opening is in the veranda (see Figure 168), an open-air room that forms the pivotal link between these two portions (see Figure 170). As it extends toward the house, part of the veranda is seen between the columns at left. The door at right leads into the garage space. Handcrafted pegged-wood detailing occurs on both the door and window casings at right. The windows are in a multi-use secondary living space (with a bathroom) attached to the garage, but accessed from the veranda. Aligned with the matching foundation wall at right, a low stone wall at left (useful for occasional extra seating) has a wide brick cap. Supporting the roof overhang, a series of square columns adapts a signature Greene & Green detail in the hand-wrought iron strapping. Rounded and stepped corbels support box beams that span the wood-paneled walkway ceiling. These cross-beams serve to unify the space, and help to offset its considerable length.

Figure 168.

VERANDA OF THE SACRAMENTO HOUSE.

The veranda overlooks the river (toward the left) and is a favorite center of family entertaining. It connects to the garage area by a covered walkway toward the right (see Figure 169). The open ceiling displays the structural elements of its hipped roof, which is spanned by trusses reinforced with metal plates. Mica-backed wall sconces with silhouetted pine trees are mounted around the area. Low brick-capped piers support pairs of square columns that are detailed with the same Greene & Greene—inspired iron strapping that appears on the columns lining the walkway to the garage. Rounded arches with "keystones" are used around the space to link the paired columns. The veranda has an outdoor kitchen built into the far wall that also helps to screen a neighboring house. Above the cooktop area is a tapering, handcrafted copper hood accented with stylized branches and leaves of hand-wrought iron. A pair of matching cupboard doors open to storage areas in the brick base below. Under the hood, the wall is faced with a slab of figured granite that matches the adjoining countertops. A sink and small refrigerator complete this area. Entry to the main house is directly opposite the outdoor kitchen. Like a compass rose, a subtle star motif is centered in a complex patterned brick-and-slate floor.

Figure 169 (right).

(CENTRAL) REAR VIEW OF THE SACRAMENTO HOUSE.

This is the primary central portion that occurs to the right of the part seen in Figure 170, which is viewed here at left. The hipped roof of the central portion contrasts with the adjoining gabled areas to either side (another similar gabled portion is out of view at right). The projecting two-story, bow-shaped bay is axially aligned with the front entry porch (seen in Figure 166). Inset between the bay's bands of windows is a series of five low-relief, hand-carved wood panels, comprising an Arts and Crafts—inspired land-scape scene. Below each of the bay's lower windows are insets of diamond-patterned shingles. The living room encompasses the bay and windows on either side (see Figure 172), with an outside door on the left side of the central bay marked by steps. Above, a second-floor hobby room at center is flanked by bedrooms. The first-floor arch-topped windows show a typical Shingle-style detail in the compressed courses above their curving tops. The terrace extends further outward here, and in the foreground, curving steps lead toward the river. A small circular window at upper left is in the den (see Figure 174). In the portion out of view at far right is a second-floor master suite, over a large first-floor library and home office area.

Figure 170 (below).

(PARTIAL) REAR VIEW OF THE SACRAMENTO HOUSE.

The home's rambling horizontal proportions and surrounding trees allowed for only incremental views. Seen from the rear, this end of the main house is where it transitions into an L-shape behind the single-story open veranda at far left (see Figure 168) toward the garage (out of view). Scenic river views guided placement of most outdoor living areas on this side. At right, massive granite-faced chimneys have brick detailing with a Prairie style influence. Between them is an intimate shade garden with a wall fountain overlooked by the dining room. Beneath an open-framed gable, a balcony adjoins the den (see Figure 174). Swiss Chalet influence is seen in railing boards with cutout edges that create a repeating pattern. Under the balcony, a beam is wrapped with iron straps at either end and supported on huge Craftsman-style brackets (knee braces). Below, a bow-shaped bay window of the breakfast area in the kitchen has an outside door (not visible, on its left side). Tapering stone piers with lanterns occur between the terrace railings. The two-story shingled wall set back to the left has arching "blind windows" with carved wood panels (see Figure 171).

Figure 171 (opposite).

REAR DETAIL OF THE SACRAMENTO HOUSE.

This is the lower and larger of two "blind windows," inset with hand-carved wood panels, that were applied to an otherwise blank, two-story shingled wall area (see Figure 170). The arch-topped casings, hand-pegged detailing, and wooden "key-tones" repeat the design of other actual windows on the house and provide additional interest, scale, and balance to the overall design. Throughout this project, the owners made it a priority to enlist the talents of numerous gifted artisans to create unique handcrafted embellishments for their home. This intricately carved high-relief panel recalls the forms of the stately old oaks that surround the house, but it may also be considered an adaptation of the "tree of life," a traditional motif that was widely interpreted in Arts and Crafts–period decorative arts. A finely detailed built-in flowerbox below is supported on three Craftsman-style brackets.

Figure 172 (above).

LIVING ROOM FIREPLACE AREA IN THE SACRAMENTO HOUSE.

A wide colonnade with brackets and through-tenon detailing frames one side of a three-part living room. On the opposite end of the room, a matching colonnade defines a similarly sized music room area. Low wainscoting, aligned with the window sills and colonnade bases, lends horizontal emphasis. Box beams and perimeter ceiling moldings also occur throughout the area. A ceiling opening in the larger central section with the bow-shaped bay (out of view at left) permits visibility of an art-glass skylight above the second floor. The opening, encircled by a railing, is at the center of a second-floor art gallery area, which adjoins the stair hall and a balcony that shelters the front door (see Figure 166). The river view is partly seen through the arched windows. Their side casings connect to a horizontal molding above, creating a panelized detail that repeats over the fireplace. A full-width wood mantel is supported by a series of slightly curving corbels. The surround is faced with matte-finished tiles in muted colors, with low-relief borders and panels that replicate period Batchelder designs. Boldly grained gumwood (an American native hardwood, not to be confused with eucalyptus) was used for all the woodwork in this area. While gumwood appeared in some early-twentieth-century interiors, its use as a finish material is uncommon today.

Figure 173.

DINING ROOM DETAIL IN THE SACRAMENTO HOUSE.

While the entire room was not yet ready to be photographed, this detail conveys a sense of its refined design and the level of its craftsmanship. Solid clear-heart redwood was used for the room's millwork, and also to create the thin wood strips woven into a diagonal basket-weave pattern on the upper walls and ceiling. This wall covering was closely replicated from one seen in the dining room of the 1902 Ehrman Mansion on Lake Tahoe, now open to the public, and part of Sugar Pine Point State Park (see Resources, page 189). Seen at lower center, "a scarf joint" (favored by Greene & Greene) is a device in which two lengths of wood are fitted to interlock, with pegs mortised through them to secure the bond. Similar pegs are used to bind the cantilevered beams comprising each corbel that extends from the wall. These support an open framework of beams, set below the ceiling level, with an octagonal configuration that adds unusual dimension to the ceiling design. Additional beams above that framework outline more inset panels of woven redwood on the ceiling.

Figure 174 (opposite).

DEN IN THE SACRAMENTO HOUSE.

Informed by the Rustic style, the design of this second-floor retreat has an open peaked ceiling. Its roughly finished beams are part of enormous triangular trusses that support the roof. Ceiling areas between the beams are clad in knotty pine, which was also used for most of the room's other woodwork. Built-in cabinets are recessed into either side of the fireplace wall, which is mostly faced with river rock. An arched inset of flatter stones is aligned with the width of the firebox. A sturdy mantel and its corbels frame a hand-carved wooden panel depicting a Native American landscape scene. The outward curve of the stone hearth repeats the arching form above the mantel. The small circular window is one of two that flank a bay window out of view at right, which adjoins an open balcony area (seen in Figures 169 and 170). Also out of view, across the room at the inside corner, is a built-in wet bar with stools. A similar open-ceiling treatment continues in a much larger, adjoining game room (out of view toward the left) with a bay window that projects from the front façade (seen on the right side of Figure 166).

Figure 175 (above).

GUEST BEDROOM IN THE SACRAMENTO HOUSE.

This room's design shows how a few simple elements, strategically placed and repeated, can create a striking overall design statement with English Arts and Crafts inspiration. Its distinctive wall treatment of linear wood moldings recalls half-timbering, set off against a contrasting textured wall covering. Guided in their placement by the room's crossing box beams, equally wide, substantial vertical posts are set against the corner walls on either side of the bed. Shaped to suggest diagonal bracing, short curving elements link the vertical posts to the wide perimeter molding adjoining the beams. Recalling a through-tenon detail, inset beveled blocks occur where each brace springs from the post, and at the intersections with a chair-rail-height banding that continues around the room.

Figure 176.

HOUSE IN SAN JOSE, CALIFORNIA.

This house is sited on a deep, level lot that allowed for a generous setback. In researching possible styles for their retirement home, the owners spotted a simple, stucco-faced, one-story bungalow in one of their resource books (The Bungalow: America's Arts & Crafts Home, by this author), which directly inspired this home. Retaining its basic configuration and proportions, the architects adapted that design in reverse (as a mirror image), and made it more emphatically Craftsman. In the course of this process, the robust single porch column went from round to square, and solid railing walls on the porch became open and squared spindled. Stone was introduced on the column's pier, and on a pair of low posts. While developing the new plans, space requirements prompted the addition of a partial second floor to the initial design. Recalling similar vintage house additions, it respects the single-story portion, and repeats its detailing for overall unity. The matching detached garage at far left is augmented by a convenient attached one that also adds more horizontality to the façade. The strip of lawn that bisects the long driveway repeats a practical period detail that absorbs staining oil drips, and also reduces the extent of pavement required.

Figure 177.

REAR OF THE SAN JOSE HOUSE.

Each side of this house was designed to stand on its own as a complete composition. The classic car now lives in the detached garage (out of view at right) adjoining the curving turnout. The upper roof's side-facing gables are highlighted here. Adapting its form and detailing from the front, a covered rear porch links the house easily to the garden, with sets of french doors open to the family room (see Figure 180). Broad steps, guarded by a watchful cat, preserve an open feeling from inside. A deck on the porch roof (see Figure 184) adjoins the master bedroom. Resembling an attached gazebo, the peaked-roof pavilion at right is topped by a weather-vane, and contains a breakfast room open to the kitchen (see Figure 181). Irregular flagstones set into the lawn contribute lively pattern to the landscape.

Figure 178.

Living Room in the San Jose House.

The living room is contained within the front-facing gable of the first floor (see Figure 176). At right, tall windows with transoms occur on three sides, admitting considerable light. Window sashes throughout utilize typical crossing, linear Craftsman designs. The front door is reflected in the large mirror (between tapering columns, seen in Figure 179). Flanked by a pair of small windows, the fireplace re-creates a period arrangement with its built-in display cabinets. Under a continuous mantel, this ensemble expresses strong horizontality. Framing the flattened peak of the fireplace opening, a low-relief tile border and "keystone" element are set against a plain tile surround and raised hearth. All of the tile reproduces period Batchelder designs in muted shades and matte finishes. Set into recessed alcoves, the small pair of windows are downlit from shallow soffits behind the crown molding. Soft, harmonious, period-style paint colors soften contrasts between wood elements and the walls.

Figure 179.

DINING ROOM (ACROSS ENTRY HALL) IN THE SAN JOSE HOUSE.

Viewed from the living room, the dining room occupies the other front corner of the house (see Figure 176) and overlooks the porch through the windows (partly seen) on the left. The other window faces toward the side. A crown molding matching that in the adjacent spaces is used with a lower picture molding in the dining room, creating a frieze area that reinforces horizontality. A strong Craftsman-style statement is made by a pair of built-in colonnades, which allow for more light and views between the two formal spaces. They also define an open hallway, the primary circulation route extending from the front door (out of view at left) to the kitchen and family room areas toward the right (see Figures 180 and 181). Repeating the linear pattern of the window sashes, overlaid wooden grids are set into the bases of the square tapering columns. Always a practical feature, a period-inspired built-in sideboard in the far right corner has a characteristic arrangement of glass-fronted china cabinet doors above a mirror-backed serving surface, with drawer and cupboard storage below. On either side are tall, tapering pilasters that echo the colonnades. At right, a swinging door opens to a butler's pantry that adjoins the kitchen.

Figure 180.

FAMILY ROOM IN
THE SAN JOSE HOUSE.

Seen from the direction of an open kitchen counter (out of view), the family room is an informal light-filled space that opens directly onto the rear porch and the garden. Its focal point is an entirely wood-paneled wall, designed with period-inspired restraint, which is centered on the fireplace. The warm wood tones complement the mottled blue-green shades of the glazed handmade tile surround and hearth, which comprise a simple arrangement of accent, border, and field tiles. Above, a shallow mantel rests on a pair of wood corbels, and a large flat-screen television is concealed behind folding wooden doors. On either side, matching arrangements of cabinets contain additional media-related storage space and components for the sound system. A pair of speakers is set into the upper cabinets. Overlaid linear detailing occurs on the recessed-panel doors.

Figure 181.

KITCHEN AND
BREAKFAST ROOM IN
THE SAN JOSE HOUSE.

This view shows how the kitchen is connected to the breakfast room (seen outside in Figure 177). At left is a side service door. The kitchen's plan includes a continuation of the sink's countertop to the right, where it makes a curving right turn (out of view) that connects to the stove area. The curving portion is also open to the family room as a bar-height serving surface. Tiled backsplash areas are accented with handmade low-relief replicas of period Batchelder designs. While first appearing to be an octagon, the breakfast room is a "nonagon" (nine-sided), which was necessary to make it work in the space. Set down two steps, it is lined with narrow french doors that open to the garden. Its all-wood ceiling has radial spoke-like beams that surround a central fixture. Parallel to its perimeter angles, hardwood flooring in the breakfast room is laid in an intriguing concentric pattern. To conserve wall space here, the refrigerator and a secondary sink were placed in an adjoining butler's pantry (to the left, out of view), which also leads to the dining room.

Figure 182.

STAIRCASE DETAIL IN THE SAN JOSE HOUSE.

*Along the central hallway, the foot of the staircase to the partial second floor can be seen from both the living and dining room. This design shows that stairs don't have to be an oversized element to make an effective statement. Handsomely detailed, the newel post and linear railing design warrant their prominent placement. Along with the house that inspired this one, the model for this design was also spotted by the owners in the same book (*The Bungalow: America's Arts & Crafts Home*), and was adapted for use here. In its original context, the railing continues up an entire staircase, which is open to one end of the living room in the 1907 Evans House in Marin County, California, designed by noted Bay Area architect Louis Christian Mullgardt. Also adapted from there is the paneling detail on the side, aligned with each step, which at the Evans House extends the full length of the staircase.*

Figure 183 (opposite).

MASTER BATHROOM DETAIL IN THE SAN JOSE HOUSE.

The period-inspired yet contemporary flair seen in the design of the master bathroom is consistent with the home's other areas. A pair of round porcelain sinks has wide flat rims with low-relief designs in a water lily motif. Their circular form guided the design of the vertical-grain white oak cabinetry, which includes an unusual detail of short, slightly bowed open spindles under the sinks. Extra open space below the curved-front drawers helps reduce the cabinet's mass and allows more limestone tile flooring to be visible, which adds a roomier feeling. Partly seen at lower right, an inlaid marble border with a stylized leaf-and-branch motif outlines the area. The built-up, stepped edge detail of the limestone slab countertop adds visual weight. Under a shallow limestone shelf, a handmade tile border is set into the stone backsplash. A pair of tall medicine cabinets, with textured glass to obscure their contents, are linked by a wooden arch and crown molding. Wall sconces light the mirror from three sides, which reflects a door to an enclosed toilet at right. Opposite but out of view is a deep spa-style tub, set into limestone-slab decking, and a large separate-stall shower.

Figure 184 (above).

MASTER BEDROOM IN THE SAN JOSE HOUSE.

Once a partial second floor became part of the plans, it provided space for a master bedroom suite plus a home office and a hobby room. The area between the living and family rooms that was initially planned for a first-floor master bedroom is now a handicapped-accessible guest suite. Open to the roof peak, the ceiling is faced entirely with narrow, natural-finish beadboard, which helps the airy space feel cozier. Side wall picture moldings add a horizontal element between the doors and windows. At left, one of three sets of french doors in this room opens to a deck over the back porch (see Figure 177). An arched accent window (one of two) recalls a feature of the vintage home that inspired this one. Set between two casement windows, the bed has delicately inlaid slats that adapt a design by Harvey Ellis, who worked briefly for Gustav Stickley. Ellis is well-known for his distinctive inlaid furniture designs produced by Stickley that combined multiple woods and metals into similar English Arts and Crafts—inspired motifs as those seen here. Out of view at left, a wall opposite the bed has a fireplace (a two-sided insert). The wall stops short of the french doors, thus allowing for access into an intimate sitting area that faces its side of the fireplace from the other side. A short hallway leading from this room to closets and the master bath is also out of view.

Figure 185 (left).

HOUSE IN CENTRAL CALIFORNIA.

Perched on a level rise with a sweeping view (to the right), this house forms an L-shape in front. The wing at left creates a partial entry courtyard effect and incorporates a recently planted olive tree. Parchment-colored stucco-faced walls have a shaded texture and aged quality that softens their presence on the open, rural acreage that includes a horse barn and a separate guest house. At center, a triple window on the partial second floor lights the staircase (see Figure 186) of the home's main portion, which is U-shaped at the back (see Figure 190). The wing at left (mostly out of view) includes a garage at its end, utility areas, plus a large art studio on a partial second floor. Extending over the front door at right, the eaves of a subtle blue-green glazed tile roof rest on a crossbeam, supported by square posts on short, tapering stone piers. Each post has paired curving brackets—inspired by the cloud-lift form favored by Greene & Greene—above crossbars, which support Craftsman-style lanterns flanking the door. Similarly detailed posts appear elsewhere (one is seen at left). Partly visible at near right, one of a pair of large stone piers, topped by lanterns, frame the front walk. These adjoin a circular front driveway turnaround with a landscaped center island (out of view).

Figure 186 (right).

STAIRCASE IN THE CENTRAL CALIFORNIA HOUSE.

The front door (partly seen at left) opens into an oversized living room with a high flat ceiling and soft green walls. First detected outside, forms and detailing that adapt period designs of Greene & Greene are in abundance on the interior. A sculptural centerpiece, the staircase was directly inspired by the one in Greene & Greene's Blacker House in Pasadena, and also displays a multitude of handcrafted joinery details. Ascending around a baby grand piano, it passes a triple window facing the front (seen in Figure 185). Numerous pegged, finger-jointed, and through-tenon details occur along its length. Occasional inlaid wood accents, in the form of small leaves, occur on the stair treads and newel post. On the side, each step is expressed as an elongated box-like form, a treatment similar to that seen on the side of the staircase in Greene & Greene's Robinson House (Figure 50). Above, a recently crafted leaded art-glass lantern hangs on a leather strap from an extended beam. Through the doorway at right (partly seen), an enclosed staircase lined with river rock runs underneath this one to a wine cellar in a partial basement. The front door and transom (fully seen in Figure 185) also utilize pegged joinery and the curving "cloud-lift" motif favored by the Greenes.

Figure 187 (opposite).

LIVING ROOM INGLENOOK IN THE CENTRAL CALIFORNIA HOUSE.

Interpreting a favorite feature of period Arts and Crafts interiors, an unusually wide inglenook frames the fireplace and anchors one end of the living room (to the left of the view in Figure 186). A deep red painted finish with a highly textured application accents this area. At far right, a narrow inset panel of leaded glass is set into a wall that screens the side of a built-in bench (one of two). Greene & Greene—inspired joinery details include pegged, overlaid cloud-lift motifs on the high bench backs, recalling the front door. Finger joints on the mantel's corners are also seen on the staircase. Enhanced by a few inlaid wood accents in the form of leaves, a small arching oak branch affixed to the mantel's face lends a delicate flourish. Pairs of stepped windows around the fireplace frame distant outlooks. Crossing linear designs in their sashes are a Craftsman-style detail that repeats throughout the home. Gathered in the vicinity by the owners, randomly sized stones and small boulders were used for the raised-hearth fireplace. Built with an arch-topped opening, its tall, tapering chimney rises to this area's peaked ceiling. The stone chimney creates an earthy backdrop for an iron chandelier. Most of the furnishings reproduce or adapt various Arts and Crafts—period designs.

Figure 188.

DINING AND KITCHEN AREA IN THE CENTRAL CALIFORNIA HOUSE.

The dining area is open to the kitchen, where an adjoining family room extends toward the right in a separate wing (seen in Figure 190). The staircase is to the left. Stone floors continue throughout this open area. A dividing colonnade has tapering columns of contrasting oak and locally grown walnut set on display cabinets. The columns support short beams with copper-covered ends that in turn support the room-wide beam above. In the kitchen, quartersawn oak cabinetry features plain recessed panels, pegged detailing, and copper hardware. Between windows, a tapering handcrafted copper hood rises above a multicolored tile panel and backsplash. Countertops are a light-colored granite. Simple glass pendant fixtures light a center island. Aligned with the island is a two-level cabinet that creates a partial screen for the kitchen, and has a bar-height copper-covered top. A ceiling fixture adapted from Greene & Greene's Duncan-Irwin House largely defines the dining area. Its small art-glass shades are hung at staggered heights from swagged chains and a wooden back-plate of crossing, layered forms. Encircling the entire dining and living area is a hand-painted frieze inspired by one in the Greenes' Thorsen House. Corner accents of stylized flowering branches are set against a plain mottled, shaded background, which continues in the remaining portions of the frieze. Wall-mounted china cabinets with sconces below occur above a large Craftsman-style sideboard, set in an alcove on the left.

Figure 189 (opposite).

MASTER BATHROOM DETAIL IN
THE CENTRAL CALIFORNIA HOUSE.

As a wall treatment, ceramic tile was exploited creatively in an alcove for an oversized pedestal tub. A large window's sweeping views are expanded by a mirrored side wall inset of matching height, which matches the proportions of another actual window, out of view on the alcove's left side. The use of so much glass in the alcove reduced the amount of costly handmade tile required. Rather than relying on even costlier tile moldings, plain field tiles provided modular flexibility for composing the panels and borders to precisely fit the areas. Tile moldings were used sparingly for the bases and caps on projecting side pilasters, which boldly frame the alcove under a panelized lintel. With a muted Arts and Crafts—inspired palette, most of the tile has a softly shaded, deep green, matte-glazed finish. Variously sized accent tiles have a bronze-like metallic glaze that reflects light. To help relate to the porcelain tub, small white tiles are used to make "dotted" outlines for the window and mirrors. To subtly engage the tub with its setting, a row of small tiles in the walls' muted color range encircle its pedestal. Limestone tile flooring extends throughout the master bath area.

Figure 190.

REAR OF THE CENTRAL CALIFORNIA HOUSE.

Glowing like a lantern in this evening view, the home has a U-shaped configuration on the back. On the partial second floor, two bedrooms each have a bathroom. Dominated by the staircase at the center (see Figure 186), the open living and dining rooms merge seamlessly with the courtyard area. Oversized sliding glass doors with strong linear divisions of Craftsman influence function like movable walls. While overhanging eaves shelter the courtyard's perimeter, there is a more significant overhang across the glass-walled end, where a pair of pendant fixtures lights an outdoor dining area. Glimpsed through the windows at far right are the family room, and the kitchen beyond. The wing at left contains the master bedroom suite, which opens onto a covered outdoor terrace across the end (out of view). The garage and studio wing (partly seen in Figure 185) extend back from behind the right side. Craftsman-style brackets occur in the gable ends.

RESOURCES

BIBLIOGRAPHY

Anderson, Timothy J; Moore, Eudora M.; Winter, Robert W. (eds.). *California Design 1910*. Pasadena, California,; California Design Publication, 1974. Reprint, Santa Barbara, Calif., and Salt Lake City, Utah: Peregrine Smith, Inc., 1980.

Cathers, David. *Gustav Stickley*. New York: Phaidon Press, Inc., 2003.

Clark, Robert Judson (ed.). *The Arts and Crafts Movement in America*. Princeton, N.J.: Princeton University Press, 1972.

Kaplan, Wendy. *"The Art That Is Life"*: *The Arts and Crafts Movement in America, 1875-1920*. Boston, Mass.: Little, Brown and Company, 1987.

Loizeaux, J.D. *Classic Houses of the Twenties*. Elizabeth, N.J.: Loizeaux Lumber Company and the Loizeaux Builders Supply Co., 1927. Reprint, Mineola, NY: The Athenaeum of Philadelphia and Dover Publications, Inc., 1992.

Massey, James and Maxwell, Shirley. *Arts & Crafts Design in America: A State-By-State Guide:* San Francisco, California: Chronicle Books, 1998.

Saylor, Henry H. *Bungalows*. New York: Robert M. McBride and Co., 1911.

Scully, Vincent. *The Shingle Style Today*. New York: George Braziller, Inc., 1974.

Sears, Roebuck and Company. *Sear, Roebuck Catalog of Houses. 1926. Chicago, IL.,* and Philadelphia, PA.: Sears and Roebuck and Company. 1926. Reprint, Mineola, NY: The Athenaeum of Philadelphia and Dover Publications, Inc., 1991.

Stickley, Gustav. *Craftsman Bungalows: 59 Homes from "The Craftsman"*. Mineola, N.Y.: Dover Publications, Inc., 1988. (Reprint of Thirty-six articles selected From issues of *The Craftsman* magazine published between December 1903 and August 1916.)

Storrer, William Allin. *The Frank Lloyd Wright Companion*. Chicago, IL: The University of Chicago Press, 1993.

Trapp, Kenneth R. (ed.). *The Arts and Crafts Movement in California: Living the Good Life*. New York: Abbeville Press Publishers, 1993.

Von Holst, Hermann Valentin. *Country and Suburban Homes of the Prairie Period.* (Originally published as: *Modern American Homes*. Chicago, IL. : American Technical Society, 1913, c.1912.) Reprint, New York: Dover Publications, Inc., 1982.

Wilson, Henry L. *California Bungalows of the Twenties*. Los Angeles, Calif., Henry L. Wilson, (n.d.) Reprint, Mineola, N.Y.: Dover Publications, Inc., 1993.

Wilson, Richard Guy. *The Colonial Revival House*. New York: Harry N. Abrams, Inc., 2004.

Winter, Robert. *The California Bungalow*. Los Angeles, Calif.: Hennessey & Ingalls, Inc., 1980.

Resources and How to Find Them

There is an ever-increasing range of architects, designers, artisans, craftspeople, workshops, and larger manufacturers who offer services or products geared to the Arts and Crafts marketplace and its design sensibility. Many of them offer their services nationally, or sell their wares by mail order or online. Others operate on a smaller scale, and prefer working on a local level. Rather that attempt to assemble a definitive list of noteworthy resources available today, we have instead opted to include a listing of those c current periodicals which feature either consistent, or occasional, coverage of Arts and Crafts-related design. Readers will find that most of today's related resources who do sell their services or wares nationally will be found as regular advertisers, and by consulting these periodicals routinely for such information, our readers will be assured of receiving the most current resource names and contact information now, and in the future. To seek out various reputable resources that operate within specific areas or individual communities only, a bit of extra sleuthing may be required. Seeking out personal referrals or recommendations from friends or acquaintances (whether for a local or nationally-available resource) is among the most reliable ways to locate them. Another route is provided by the internet, which provides access to a vast variety of resources.

AMERICAN BUNGALOW
123 South Baldwin Ave
P.O. Box 756
Sierra Madre, CA 91025-0756
(800) 350-3363
www.americanbungalow.com

ARTS & CRAFTS HOMES AND THE REVIVAL

C/o Gloucester Publishers
108 East Main Street
Gloucester, MA 01930
(800) 462-0211
www.artsandcraftshomes.com

OLD HOUSE INTERIORS

C/o Gloucester Publishers
108 East Main Street
Gloucester, MA 01930
(800) 462-0211
www.oldhouseinteriors.com

OLD HOUSE JOURNAL

C/o Restore Media, LLC
1000 Potomac Street NW, Suite 102
Washington, DC 20007
(800) 234-3797
www.oldhousejournal.com

PERIOD HOMES

69-A Seventh Ave
Brooklyn, NY 11217
(718) 636-0788
www.period-homes.com

STYLE: 1900

333 North Main Street
Lambertville, NJ 08530
(690) 397-4104
www.style1900.com

PRESERVATION RESOURCE

All readers of this book are strongly encouraged to support the critical and ongoing cause of America's historic preservation. The National Trust for Historic Preservation, a private nonprofit organization chartered by Congress in 1949, is dedicated to the protecting the irreplaceable, and fighting to save historic buildings and the neighborhoods they anchor. The National Trust's programs and publications are made possible in part by membership dues and contributions. Among the benefits of membership are free admission to many important historic house museums and sites operated by the National Trust across the country. The trust's own bi-monthly periodical, *Preservation*, covers diverse topics of interest to both owners and admirers of America's historic homes and sites from throughout our history. While *Preservation*

does not routinely focus on the Arts and Crafts period, it is nevertheless an important and valuable resource for its coverage of fascinating historic sites, and also of today's current and critical preservation issues. Please note that all subscriptions to *Preservation* are obtained as a benefit of membership to the National Trust.

PRESERVATION

C/o The National Trust For Historic Preservation
Membership Department
1785 Massachusetts Avenue NW
Washington, DC 20036
(800) 944-6847
Email: members@nthph.org
www.Preservationonline.org

BOOK RESOURCE

The following is a comprehensive source for books related to aspects of the Arts and Crafts Movement. A mail order catalog is available by request. Proceeds of these book sales also help to support the ongoing maintenance of the Gamble House, an American Arts and Crafts masterpiece by architects Greene and Greene, which is open to the public as a house museum. Located on the premises, the Gamble House bookstore is housed in the original garage designed by the architects.

The Gamble House Bookstore
4 Westmoreland Place
Pasadena, CA 91103
(626) 449-4178
www.gamblehouse.org/bookstore/

Historic House Museums and Related Sites

The following sites are open to the public as house museums or historic sites, and their appearance (or place of reference) in this book is noted for each. Most house museums have docents on hand to lead public tours, and some may offer self-guided tours. Usually a consequence of limited funding and volunteer staffing, many locations have rather limited days and hours of operation, and some may require advance reservations for all tours. When planning visits for large groups, it is important to make all arrangements well ahead of time. To avoid disappointment, it is strongly recommended that the *current* open day(s) and

hours of operations of any historic site should be confirmed shortly in advance of any visit, as these may be subject to change without notice. By special prior arrangements, some locations may be opened to visitors (sometimes for larger groups only) at alternate times. Some of these house museums, and/or their grounds, may be available for rent as venues for special private events. Because these historic sites are sustained mostly through tax-deductible donations, it is important to give them ongoing support through visits, referrals to friends, and by membership in their parent organizations. Other ways to contribute can include volunteering time, professional services, or other special skills. Not only as sources of insight and learning, these sites are simply enjoyable to experience in person.

AINSLEY HOUSE (Figures 99-102)

300 Grant Street
Campbell, CA 95008
(408) 866-2119
www.ci.campbell.ca.us/communityandarts/
ainsleyhouse.htm

GEORGE BARTON HOUSE (Figure 60)

(part of the Darwin D. Martin House Complex)
118 Summit Avenue (George Barton House)
125 Jewett Parkway (Darwin D. Martin House)
Buffalo, NY 14214
(716) 856-3858
www.darwinmartinhouse.org

BOETTCHER MANSION (Figures 116-119)

900 Colorow Road
Golden, CO 80401
(303) 526-0855
www.co.jefferson.co.us/ext/dpt/comm_res/boettcher/
contact.htm

GRAYCLIFF (Figures 79-82)

Isabel R. Martin House and Estate
6472 Old Lake Shore Road
Derby, New York 14047
(716) 947-9217
www.graycliff.bfn.org

LANTERMAN HOUSE (Figures 31-36)

4420 Encinas Drive
La Cañada Flintridge, CA 91011
(818) 790-1421
www.lacanadaflintridge.com

CRAFTSMAN FARMS (referenced on pages 13-14)

Stickley Museum
2352 Route 10 West
Parsippany, NJ 07950
(973) 540-1165
www.stickleymuseum.org

EHRMAN MANSION (referenced in

caption of Figure 173)
Sugar Pine Point State Park
Highway 89 (west side of Lake Tahoe)
P.O. Box 266
Tahoma, CA 96142
(916) 525-7982
www.parks.ca.gov

FOREST HILL CLUB HOUSE (Figure 107)

c/o Forest Hill Association
381 Magellan Street
San Francisco, CA 94116
(415) 664-0542
Note: While not routinely open to the public, the
Forest Hill Club House invites inquires about its availability for rent as a special events venue.

GAMBLE HOUSE (referenced on pages 56-57)

4 Westmoreland Place
Pasadena, CA 91103
(626) 793-3334
www.gamblehouse.org

PLEASANT HOME (referenced on pages 79-80)

(John Farson House)
c/o Pleasant Home Foundation
217 Home Ave
Oak Park, IL 60302
(708) 383-2654
www.pleasanthome.org

PURCELL-CUTTS HOUSE (referenced on page 89)

2328 Lake Place
Minneapolis, MN 55405
(612) 870-3131
www.artsmia.org/unified-vision/purcell-cutts-house/

ROYCROFT CAMPUS (referenced on pages 13-14)

(vicinity of Main and South Grove Street)
c/o Roycroft Campus Corporation
One RoycroftCampus
P.O. Box 743
East Aurora, NY 14052
(716) 655-0261
www.roycroftcampuscorporation.com

A ROYCROFT NOTE: Comprised of fourteen original structures, the historic Roycroft community's campus survives largely intact, and is a must-see destination for all Arts and Crafts devotees. Not to be missed is the Elbert Hubbard Roycroft Museum, named for the community's founder, housed in a nearby 1910 Craftsman style bungalow. The Roycroft Campus Corporation ("RCC"), a non-profit organization whose goal is a complete reunification of all surviving Roycroft buildings under a single, visionary stewardship, is guiding the long-term future of the campus. At this time, the 1902 Copper Shop is open to the public as a visitor's center and gallery for Roycroft Renaissance artisans. The RCC envisions the campus of the future as a major cultural tourism destination, and once again a vital, working community of master craftspeople, as well as a study center for the American Arts and Crafts movement. Support of the RCC's efforts is welcome through active (and tax-deductible) membership. A campus landmark and ideal base for exploring this area's rich history, the 1905 Roycroft Inn is a recently resorted, full-service hotel. Among nearby Buffalo's many architectural treasures is Frank Lloyd Wright's Darwin D. Martin House complex, which includes the George Barton House (Figure 60). Also by Wright is the Martin's summer home, Graycliff (Figures 79-82) in nearby Derby, on Lake Erie.

ELBERT HUBBARD ROYCROFT MUSEUM

363 Oakwood Avenue
East Aurora, NY
(716) 652-4735
www.roycrofter.com/museum.htm

ROYCROFT INN (referenced on page 14)

40 South Grove Street
East Aurora, NY 14052
(716) 652-5552
www.roycroftinn.com

Credits
PHOTO CREDITS
Thanks to Action Photo of Concord, CA for their expert help with photo processing; Figures 11-12 from the collection of Paul Duchscherer; Figures 1, 14–17, and 61 appear courtesy of Dover Publications, Inc.

MISCELLANEOUS CREDITS
Figure 3: Restoration architect: Jeff Miller, General contractor: Green Gables/Lindley Morton; Figure 5: interior millwork restoration and wood finishing: Craftsman Design and Renovation, Stencil design by

Trimbelle River Studio; Figure 6: Renovation architect: Steve Routon, Metal gate designed and made by Kenneth B. Wright; Figure 9: interior design and decorative painting scheme concept and execution: C.J. Hurley Century Arts, Stained glass work and metalwork detailing (buffet sconces, repousse' roses, and hammered ceiling medallions) designed and crafted by C.J. Hurley; Figure 10: restoration architect: Mary Wilkinson/Wilkinson Designworks, Landscape designer: Steve Mascari/Westwind Landscape; Figure 13: Renovation architect: Larry Johnson, principal/The Johnson Partnership, General contractor: Alan Thorslund/Northwest Housewrights; Figure 19, Renovation architect: Allen J. Zimmer/Architects West, General contractor: Steve Crawford/Crawford Construction, Project interior designer: Paul Duchscherer*; Landscape designer: Suxan Van Atta/Van Atta Associates, Art glass (at front door): Brian McNally; Special thanks to Bruce Irving and Russell Morash of the PBS series *This Old House* (Figure 19 was that program's Winter 2000 project); Figures 25-29: Exterior paint colors: Bennett Christopherson AIA, Landscape design and installation: Shawn E. Hall Designs, Interior design consultant: Bonnie Ross Staging and Interiors, Interior paint colors: Paul Duchscherer*, Fireplace tile: RTK Studios, Art glass: Stained Glass Garden, Curtains and Pillows: Dianne Ayres*/Arts & Crafts Period Textiles, Pottery made by Ramah Commanday, Period lighting: Omega Too, Kitchen sink: Ohmega Salvage, Stove: Apple Antiques, Reproduction furniture sources: The Craftsman Home, Caldonia Studios, Warren Hile Studios; Figure 30: Pergola rebuilt by Ronin Builders/Robert Clemens, Paint colors: Four Dimensions design; Figures 31-32: Exterior restoration: John Benriter and Rich Caruso; Figure 34: Mural restoration: Bob Burchman and Ed Pinson/Landmark Painted Design and Restoration: Figures 33, 35 and 36: Decorative painting restoration: Bob Burchman and Ed Pinson/Landmark Painted Design and Restoration; Master bedroom wallpaper reproduction: Carter & Company; Wallpaper installation: Phillip Ostler; Figure 37: Paint colors: Erik Hanson and Beth Montes; Figure 38: Renovation architect: Christopher Ward, General contractor: Max Dial, Landscaping contractor: Victor Lang; Figures 39-42: General contractor: Tom Lewis, Lighting: Brass Light Gallery, and Rejuvenation Lighting and House Parts, Fireplace mantle restoration: Erik Hanson, Wallpaper: Bradbury & Bradbury Art Wallpapers*, Dining room furniture made by Walt Diebold, Dining room woodwork repair: Robert Goe, Woodwork restoration: Gary (Butch) Babb, Built-in sideboard lights: Jim Gibson, Kitchen design consultant: Bill Jones, Kitchen cabinets made by Bob Stewart, Stove restored by Pacific Stove Works, Rear terrace design consultant: Bill Jones, Fireplace tiles: Laird Plumleigh/Alchemie Studios, Landscape architect: Gary McCook; Figure 43: Restoration architect: Martin Eli

Weil, Figures 45-48: Renovation architect: Randell L. Makinson, dining room fixture designed by Randell L. Makinson; Figure 49: Landscape design by Phaedra Ledbetter; Figure 50: Reproductions of original entry hall furniture by Anthony Fortner; Figure 51: Reproduction of original den firebox and mantel by Jeff Grainger; Figure 52: Kitchen design (including cabinets and ceiling light/pot rack design) by Phaedra Ledbetter, Cabinets made by Brian Krueger, Ceiling light/pot rack made by Jeff Grainger; Figure 53: Sliding door designed by Phaedra Ledbetter and made by Constantino Fine Furniture; Figure 55: Pool area designed by Phaedra Ledbetter and constructed by California Pools of Pasadena/Mike Sorenson; Figures 56-59: General contractor: Jeffrey Pollard/Pollard construction, Interior Designer: Su Bacon/Historic Lighting, Inc., Furnishings and Lighting: Historic Lighting, Inc., Art glass: Brian McNally, Tile: Mission Tile West, colors (wood and walls): Trinity Construction, Landscaping: Charles Phillips, Electrical work: John Watson/Watson Electrical; Figure 63: Wallpaper frieze (foreground): Bradbury & Bradbury Art Wallpapers*, Stair well wallpaper: Trustworth Studios, Carpet runner: J.R. Burrows & Company; Figure 64: Wallpaper: Bradbury & Bradbury Art Wallpapers*; Figure 68: Iron firescreen designed and made by Michael Manzavrakos; Figures 69-74: Renovation architect: Sala Architects, Inc./Joseph G. Metzler, AIA and Steve Buetow, AIA, General contractor: Aulick & Luloff, Contractor for front terrace and steps: Peter Vujovich, Landscape designer: Dennis Piermont, Landscape contractor: Robert Reynolds; Figure 78: Curtains by Prairie Textiles from Ann Wallace, new furniture by L. and J.G. Stickley, Inc.; Figures 85-86: Kitchen remodel architects and dining room furniture design: Vetter Denk Architects/John Vetter, kitchen cabinetry, millwork, bay window, built-ins, and dining room table fabrication: C. A. Chandler/Charles Chandler, Dining chairs made by John Vetter; Figure 87: Renovation architect: Rynerson O'Brien Architecture/Stephen Rynerson*, partner in charge, Project managers: Janet McFarland and Jack McGuire, General contractor: Alan Taylor; Figure 88: Renovation architect: Rynerson O'Brien Architecture/Steven Rynerson*, partner in charge, with Larry Axelrod, project manager, General contractor: Landmark Builders/Jaime Stewart and Todd McElvain, partners: Cabinet work: Bill Eichenberger*; Figures 90-91: Wallpaper: Bradbury & Bradbury Art Wallpapers*, Carpets: J. R. Burrows & company: Figures 94-97: Renovation architect: Randell L. Makinson, Interior design consultation: Su Bacon/Historic Lighting, Inc., Furnishings and lighting: Historic Lighting, Inc., Colors (wood and walls): Brian Miller, Tile maker: Diana Watson/Crager Tile, Tile restoration: Sheila Osborne, Electrical work: John Watson/Watson Electrical, Carpentry: Denise Cheseny, and Lightfoot

Studios/Scott Lightfoot and Mike Banks, Landscaping: Kari Aspens, Plumbing work: Ron Ives, Flooring restoration: Steve Johnston, Art glass: Judson Studios, Plastering: Randy Ayers, gutters: Amidou Diakite/Le Petite Sheet Metal; Figures 103-106: General contractor: Peter Vujovich/Vujovich Design Guild, Decorative painting: Gwen Hauser, Wallpaper: Bradbury & Bradbury Art Wallpapers*; Figure 108: General Contractor: Paul Anderson; Figures 110-114: Custom and period furniture: Fred Johns/Now and Then Antiques; Kitchen general contractor: Winans Construction/Paul and Nina Winans*; Figure 115: Remodel architect: Osburn Design/Steve Osburn, General contractor: Neil Yellin; Figures 116-119: Renovation architect: Long-Hoeft Architects, General Contractor: T.C.2, Figure 117: Lighting: Rejuvenation Lighting & House Parts, Reproduction furniture: L & J.G. Stickley, Inc.; Figures 120-135: Renovation architect: John E. Matthams, General contractor: De Mattei Construction/Mark De Mattei, Project manager: Kirk Powell, Master carpenter: Chuck Brown, Overall project designer (interior and exterior areas) and color consultant: Paul Duchscherer*, Landscaping contractor/designer: Irving Tamura/Tamura Designs, Inc., with Landscape design consultant: Paul Duchscherer*, Exterior and interior painting/restoration: Magic Brush, Inc./Robert Durfort*, Exterior/shingle staining and interior mill-work restoration and finishing: Steve Peterson, Art glass in windows, skylight, cabinetry, and lighting designed and made by Ted Ellison/Theodore Ellison Designs*, Dining room lighting fixtures' woodwork by Trevor Davis, Family room TV's folding doors (over fireplace), parlor center table and adjacent cabinet designed and crafted by Debey Zito, with hand carvings by Terry Schmitt/Debey Zito Fine Furniture* and handcrafted metalwork by Audel Davis, Fireplace tile installations: Riley Doty/Doty Tile*, Living room fireplace tile made by Diane Winters/Winters Tileworks*, family room window-seat fabric and matching pillows by Archive Edition Textiles, living room ceiling fixture and wall sconces by Michael Adams/Aurora Studios, master bedroom, guest bedroom and guest bathroom curtains and pillows made by Dianne Ayres/Arts & Crafts Period Textiles*, guest bedroom and master bedroom wallpaper: Bradbury & Bradbury Art Wallpapers*, Wallpaper installation: Peter Bridgman*; Figures 136-139: Renovation architect: James D. McCord, AIA, General contractor: Bill Jetton/Jetton Construction, Inc., Landscape design, Jim Dixon, Brick work: R. H. Darling/Across the Pond Construction, lanterns: Old California Lantern Company, Tile design and installation: Riley Doty/Doty Tile*, Driveway gate design and manufacture: Joseph Mross/Archive Designs, Tile artist (on driveway gate columns): Stuart Compton*, Tile layout: Diane Winters/Winters Tileworks*; Figures 140-146: Renovation architect: Mark Tarasuck, AIA and Associates, General contractor and millwork: Tony E.

Parker General Builders, Flooring: Woodchuck Flooring, Tile Work: C. J. Tile Company, Tile Artist: Laird Plumleigh/Achemie Studios, Painting: Gilbert's Painting; Figures 147-156: Renovation architect: Jim Logan, General contractor: Rich Jorgensen, Tom Lewis, cabinetmaker and master woodworker, Landscape architect: Jack Gear; Figure 157: Builder: Brad Hall/Kupono Construction, Landscaping: John Majewski; Figure 158: Architect: G. Robert Mahrt, General Contractor: Boa Constructors/John Colgan and Jim Walker; Figure 159: Architect: The Johnson Partnership/Larry Johnson, Principal, and Howard Miller, project architect, General contractor: Tip Top Homes, Inc./Mike Bohannon, Landscape architect: Glenn Takagi; Figures 160-163: Architect: Jarvis architects/Glen Jarvis, principal, Project architect: Ed Buchanan, General contractor: The Summerwood Company/Scott Cameron; Figures 164-165: Architecture and landscape design: Stephen Adams/Adams Design Associates, Inc.; Figures 166-175: General contractor: Aspeotis Construction/Tom Aspeotis, Overall project (exterior and interior) design consultant: Paul Duchscherer*, Interior furnishings selection and procurement: Virginia Sewell/Scofield's Furniture; Figure 166: Stone mason: George Becerra, Carpenter: Norm Boden, Art glass (at far right): Ted Ellison/Theodore Ellison Designs*, Figure 167: Carpenter: Craig Patterson, Stone mason: George Becerra; Figure 168: Carpenters: Norm Boden and Craig Patterson, Copper and wrought iron work: Larry Meeks; Figure 169-171: Carpenter: Doug Neto; Figure 179: Carpenter: Doug Neto; Figure 170-171: Wood carving: Ian Agrell/Agrell & Thorpe, Ltd.; Figure 172: Plaster: Nick Hagopian, Hardware: Chris Efker/Craftsman Hardware; Figure 173: Carpenter: Doug Neto, Millwork and cabinetry: Ron Garcia and Jim Miller, Art glass (out of view): Larry Davis; Figure 174: Carpenter: Dean Schottsky, Wood carving: Ian Agrell/Agrell & Thorpe, Ltd.; Figure 175: Carpenter: Paul Walker, Art Glass (out of view): Larry Davis; Figures 176-184: Architecture and interior design: Garcia Teague/Gil Garcia and Wendy Teague, General Contractor: Frank Prats; Figure 184: Bed made by Voorhees Craftsman; Figures 185-190: Architect: J. D. Morrow & Associates, Builder: Patron Construction Company, Interior Design: Jan Davidson, Interior & lighting consultation: Su Bacon/Historic Lighting, Inc., Cabinetry: Pete Thomsen/Pacific Valley Woodsmith, Mantel, staircase and adjacent lantern crafted by Pete Thomsen and Jan Davidson, Coppersmith: Joseph Mross/Archive Designs, Decorative Painting; Gloria Fisher, Landscaping: Martin Aguilera, Masonry: Brad Bartholomay Landscape Stone & Masonry, Tile installation: Lindsey Alberts/DL Tile, Tile manufacturers: Handcraft Tile, Tile Collection, Mission Tile West.

*Individuals or businesses who are members of Artistic License; www.artisticlicense.org

ACKNOWLEDGMENTS

We are grateful for the many people who helped us to make this book project a reality. Due to space limitations, not all homes that were photographed could be included. Most examples were found through networking, and sometimes by sheer serendipity. Because our travel and photography schedule was tightly timed, a few quick decisions were made to take an unplanned photograph on the spot. While we met some homeowners this way, or were able to track them down later, we were unable to contact all of them. Nevertheless, we are most grateful for such unplanned contributions, and extend special thanks to anyone who may be surprised to find their home included. We also apologize in advance to anyone else whose name has been inadvertently omitted. While many of the following are homeowners, others are supportive friends, colleagues, and acquaintances. Each helped us out in various ways for this project.

Stephen Adams/Adams Design Associates, Inc., American Bungalow/John Brinkman and staff, Holly and Stuart Rosenblum, Terry Anderson, Artistic License, Dianne Ayres and Timothy Hansen/Arts & Crafts Period Textiles, Su Bacon/Historic Lighting and staff, Steve Bauer/Bradbury & Bradbury Art Wallpapers and staff, Arlene Baxter/Berkeley Hills Realty and David Mostardi, Barry Berg, John Benriter, Berkeley Architectural Heritage Association/Anthony Bruce, David E. Berman/Trustworth Studios, Robert Blake, Bruce Bradbury, Karen Brey/Campell Historical Museum & Ainsley House, Jane Browne and Celeste Rue, John Burrows and Dan Cooper/J.R. Burrows & Company, Terri and Scott Cameron/The Summerwood Company, Julie Castiglia/The Castiglia Agency, Century Arts/C.J. Hurley and Barbara Pierce, Kathy and Roger Chase, Ann and Andre Chaves, Mary and William Chenoweth, Dee and Steve Ciancio/The Crafted Home, Brian Coleman and Howard Cohen, Tim Counts and Mike Lazaretti/Twin Cities Bungalow Club, Doria and Scott Colner, The Craftsman Farms Foundation, Jan and Tom Davidson/Tyler and Wyatt Davidson, Holly and David Davis, Linda Deaktor, Jan and Americo Del Calzo, Riley Doty, Leon F. Drozd, R. Geraldine Duchscherer, Kenneth J. Duchscherer, Steven P. and Sandy Wynn Duchscherer, Diane and Robert Dufault, Ed and Mary Lu Edick/Village Properties, Theodore Ellison, Judy Epstein and Rick Wiliams, Nick Ericson, Sally Fisher, George Fleerlage, Roger Fong and Erik Kramvik, Judy Freed and Barry Hemphill, Kevin Frisch, Candy Galvan, Gamble House/Edward R. Bosley and staff, Gibbs Smith, Publishers/Gibbs Smith, Suzanne Taylor Christopher Robbins, Madge Baird, and Jennifer Maughan, David Goldberg, Foster Goldstrom, Lisa Goodman, Glen Gormezano, Robert Gould, Jean Gould Bryant, and Richard Gould, Vicki Granowitz and William Lees, Graycliff Conservancy, Inc./Reine Hauser and Susan Ryan, Julie Greenberg, Jeff Gumpert, Mel and Shirley Gumpert, Carol and Jim Hansen, Carlen Hatala, Ingrid Helton and Erik Hanson, Rob and Rawn Henry, James Heuer and Robert Mercer, Denise, Keith, and Stephanie Hice, Historic Seattle, Cathy and Steve Hoelter, Dard Hunter III, Mary Ann Huchison and Ben Davis, Glen Jarvis and Ed Buchanan/Jarvis Architects, Lee Jester and Michelle Nelson/The Craftsman Home, Wade Joffrion, Bruce Johnson/Grove Park Inn Arts & Crafts Conference, Lani and Larry Johnson and Howard Miller/The Johnson Partnership, Jan Johnston and David Greer, Douglas Keister, Julie and Bill Kennedy, Ellen and Harvey Knell, Louise Kodis and David Glass, Lorna Kollmeyer, Larry Kreisman and Wayne Dodge, Craig A. Kuhns, Debra Ware and Ed Pinson/Landmark Painted Design & Restoration, Phaedra and Mark Ledbetter, Lamar Lentz, Sarah and Michael LeValley, Lisa and Ray Lewis, Suzy Spafford Lidstrom and Ray Lidstrom, Michelle and Malcolm Liepke, Boice Lydell, Helen and Stanley Lindwasser, Arlene and Don Magdanz, Randell L. Makinson, Mark Mansfield and Juliana Moore, Suzanne and Paul Markham, Janet Mark and Terry Geiser, John Martine, Vonn Marie May, Pam McClary and Robert Rust, Karen and Bob McCrary, Cynthia Shaw McLaughlin/Boettcher Mansion/Colorado Arts & Crafts Society, Brian McNally, Jon and Steve Melkerson, Dr. Mike Metros, Laura Meyers, Amy Miller/Trimbelle River Studio, Geri and John Miner, Randi and Steve Moore, Beth and Zeke Montes, Joseph Mross/Archive Designs, Cyril I. Nelson, Old House Interiors/Patricia Poore and staff, Cody Oreck and Bruce Oreck, Pasadena Heritage, Karen and Tom Paluch, Melissa Patten/Lanterman House, Period Homes and Traditional Building/Clem Labine and staff, Marsha Perloff, Mark J. Peszko, Catherine and Lewis Phelps, Laurie Taylor/Ivy Hill Interiors, Frank Pond, Bonnie Poppe, Peter Post, Jane Powell, David Raposa and Ed Trosper/City Living Realty, Cheryl Robertson, The Roycroft Inn/Martha B. Augat and staff, Melodie and Chris Rufer, Steve Rynerson and Pat O'Brien/Rynerson O'Brien Architecture and staff, Martha and Thom Sandberg, San Francisco Heritage/Natasha Glushkoff, Save Our Heritage Organization (San Diego), Connie and Mark Saverino, Debbie and Dennis Segers, Marjory H. Sgroi/Ashton-Drye Associates, Charles Shanabruch/Historic Chicago Bungalow Asssociation, Phyllis and Thomas Shess, Sandra Simpson/Metropolitan Realty, Bruce Smith and Yoshiko Yamamoto/The Arts & Crafts Press, Julie and Rex Smith, Marcia Smith, Vivian Smolke and Frank Naso, Debbie and John Stall, Sandra and Michael Starks, Vivian Steblay, Ray Stubblebine, Style 1900/David Rago, Marilyn Fish and staff, Pat Suzuki, Marc Tarasuck and Associates, Marty and Ron Thomas, Cynthia Thompson, Laura Mercier Thompson/Pleasant Home, Kitty Turgeon, Jenni and John Vetter, Elder and Gladys Vides/Painting Concepts, Martin Eli Weil, Kathleen West, West Adams Historical Association, Linda and Robert Willett, Winans Construction/Paul and Nina Winans, Jan Winford, Diane Winters, Arlene Wright and Derek Vanderlinde, Kay and Harold Wright, Dr. Robert Von Gunten, Mary Ann and Steve Voorhees/Voorhees Craftsman, Linda Yeomans/Historic Preservation Planning & Design, Debey Zito and Terry Schmitt, Monica and Matthew Zuck. Special appreciative thanks to Jeff Weathers, Don Merrill and Fumi Momota, for their ongoing supportiveness, and especially to John Freed, who is always willing to share his invaluable opinions, energetic guidance, and solid encouragement. We salute you!

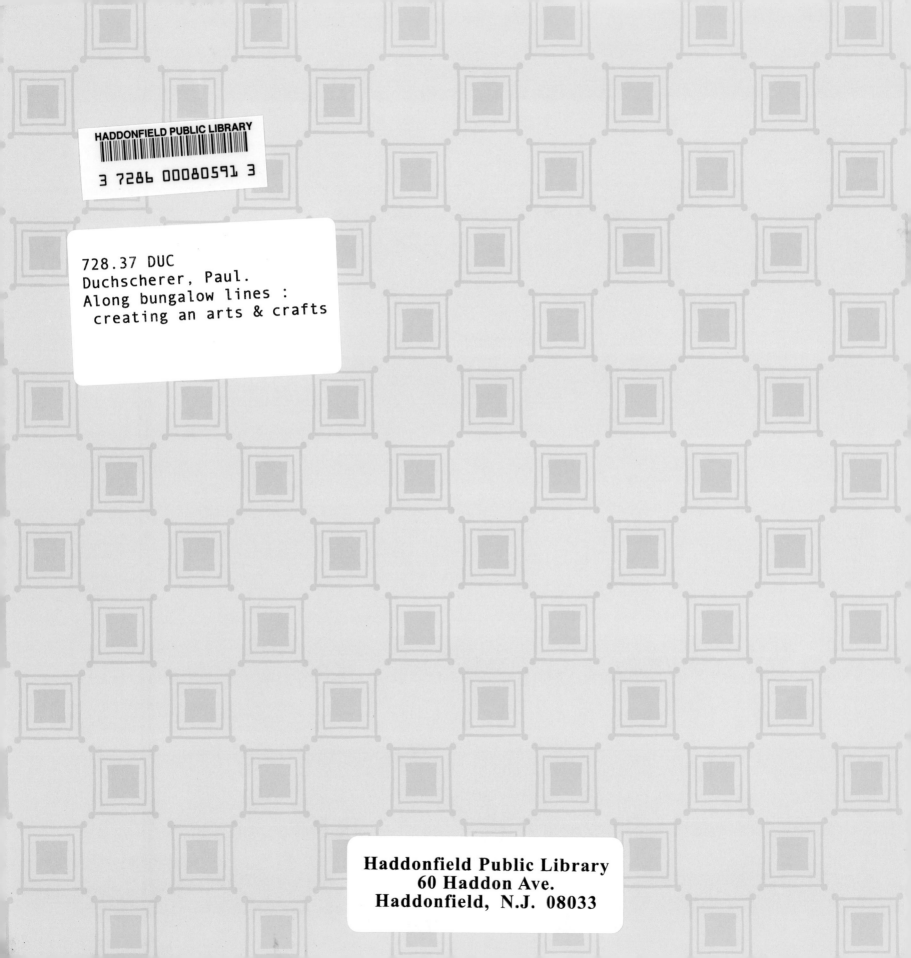